The End

the dogs, the woman enlisted the advice of her favorite NASCAR driver, Ryan Newman, and his wife Krissie. She had seen television interviews with the couple about their love for animals, and the woman thought that if anyone could help her, the Newmans could. The Newmans paid a local veterinarian to spay/neuter and vaccinate all the dogs. Krissie drove to the woman's home with her assistant, Michelle Croom, and two employees of the Humane Society of Catawba County's no-kill shelter. They took the majority of the dogs to the shelter, where all were adopted within a few months time. The family kept four of the dogs, which had been spayed and neutered so the family would never be in the position to care for an unwanted litter of puppies again. The family was extremely grateful for the Newmans' generosity, and they remain in touch.

Ryan and Krissie realized that they could not take financial responsibility for every family in a similar situation; however, they wanted to make sure that communities across the nation could provide the much-needed services of no-kill animal shelters and public low-cost spay/neuter clinics. They asked me to help them establish the Ryan Newman Foundation so they could provide education and funding to nonprofit organizations who could offer these services in their own communities.

An avid fisherman, Ryan also wanted the foundation to focus on conservation and the responsible management and use of natural resources. Additionally, Ryan wanted to continue to support the Rich Vogler Scholarship because he had received that scholarship to attend Purdue University, where he graduated with a degree in vehicle structure engineering.

And so the Ryan Newman Foundation was established in January 2005 by Ryan and Krissie Newman. The foundation strives to educate and encourage people to spay/neuter their dogs and cats and to adopt pets from animal shelters; to educate children and adults about the importance of conservation so the beauty of the great outdoors can be appreciated by future generations; and to provide college scholarship funding through the Rich Vogler Scholarship program to students interested in auto racing careers.

If you would like to read about the Ryan Newman Foundation, including the latest news about Ryan and Krissie's philanthropic efforts, we invite you to visit our website at www.ryannewman foundation.org.

Thank you for supporting the Ryan Newman Foundation by purchasing *Pit Road Pets*. 🐾

Above: HSCC's current shelter operates from old outdoor kennels and a makeshift garage. The staff struggles to keep the animals warm in winter and cool in summer.

Left: The new 14,000 sq. ft. indoor multipurpose facility will contain a no-kill shelter, education center and spay/ neuter clinic.

Pit Road Pets
NASCAR Stars and Their Pets

Photography by   Written by
Karen Will Rogers   Laura Lacy

A Ryan Newman Foundation Publication

This edition of *Pit Road Pets™: NASCAR Stars and Their Pets*
first published in 2006 by the Ryan Newman Foundation,
P.O. Box 5998, Statesville, NC 28687.

Publisher: Ryan Newman Foundation (Ryan and Krissie Newman)
Project Manager: Rosalie De Fini
Photographer: Karen Will Rogers
Writer: Laura Lacy
Editor: Amy McCauley
Assistant Editor: Beth Hardy
Design and Print Production: Dina Dembicki Graphic Design
Logo Designer: Lori Munro

Ryan Newman Foundation
P.O. Box 5998
Statesville, NC 28687
www.ryannewmanfoundation.org

Pit Road Pets
www.pitroadpets.com
info@pitroadpets.com

100% of the Ryan Newman Foundation's portion of the net proceeds from this book will be donated to the Humane Society of Catawba County's capital campaign to build a no-kill animal shelter, education center, dog park and regional public low-cost spay/neuter clinic in Hickory, North Carolina. The facility will serve the region from the mountains to the piedmont of North Carolina, which encompasses the heart of NASCAR country.

The Ryan Newman Foundation is a 501(c)(3) nonprofit organization.

This book is dedicated to the abandoned and homeless pets at animal shelters across the world.

Contents

Contents

Foreword

by Ryan and Krissie Newman

When we're not at the racetrack, our life is spent in the company of dogs. We don't consider our dogs to be "just pets." To us, they are family. We can't imagine what our lives would be like without Digger, Harley, Mopar and Socks. They sleep with us at night, and they spend the day with us – whether that means fishing at the pond on our property or hanging out at the office. When life is stressful, the dogs make us smile and remember that family is what is important in life. When we're feeling sick, the dogs cuddle with us on the sofa to try to make us feel better. They love us unconditionally.

All of our dogs were rescued. The joy they bring to our lives inspired us to get involved with the Humane Society of Catawba County, where we live in North Carolina. Krissie volunteered for their board of directors, and both of us have served as the honorary chairs of their capital campaign to build a new no-kill animal shelter, education center, dog park and regional public low-cost spay/neuter clinic. This facility will serve people from the mountains to the foothills of North Carolina, which is the heart of NASCAR country.

By volunteering at the local humane society, we learned even more about the enormous problem of pet overpopulation in our country. We were shocked and saddened to find out that approximately 9.7 million dogs and cats are euthanized in our nation each year just because there are not enough homes out there for all the abandoned animals.

We felt it was important to volunteer at our local humane society because we can all make a difference if we start in our own backyard. But we wanted to do even more, so in January 2005 we started the Ryan Newman Foundation. The NASCAR community and fans have been very supportive of our foundation and of this *Pit Road Pets* book project. We receive so many e-mails and letters from fans who love animals and are glad to see the work we are doing through our foundation. Many NASCAR drivers and team members are animal lovers, so we thought this book would be a great opportunity to give the fans a look into the lives of their favorite drivers and the pets they love.

We would like to thank all of the drivers, team members and media personalities who took time out of their busy schedules to participate in this book. We would also like to thank all the NASCAR fans who have supported our cause by purchasing this book. The Ryan Newman Foundation will donate 100% of our net proceeds from the sale of this book to the Humane Society of Catawba County's capital campaign.

Pets are wonderful additions to a family. If you are thinking about adding a pet to your family, please consider adopting a homeless animal from your local animal shelter; and please spay or neuter your pets to reduce the number of unwanted puppies and kittens born each year. Together we can make a difference – one animal at a time!

Introduction

by Laura Lacy and Karen Will Rogers

NASCAR is the largest spectator sport in America and has the most extraordinary fans. How do NASCAR stars manage to live life in the fast lane ten months out of the year yet maintain their momentum? Most will tell you it has everything to do with the foundation and support of their families – including their pets. The love and joy these animals bring to their overloaded lives keeps these NASCAR stars going when the going gets tough. When they open that door to their motorcoaches after a tough day at the track, their world brightens with a warm, wet-nosed greeting from their furry children. In *Pit Road Pets*, you'll experience the effect these comforting creatures have on the lives of their daredevil owners and how they enhance their hectic lifestyles.

This special group of animal-loving NASCAR stars wants very much to see the national animal overpopulation problem reduced dramatically. Our nation is in trouble. The problem is at epidemic proportions as animals are euthanized every day due to our society's negligence. Our nation's animal shelters and humane societies work tirelessly to make sure these abandoned animals are placed in loving homes.

If you would like to help, please consider making a donation to or volunteering at your local animal shelter, or visit the Ryan Newman Foundation website (www.ryannewmanfoundation.org) for more information. Funding and volunteer hours are always needed to operate these life-saving facilities.

The golden rule applies to animals as it does to people: it is important to show animals the same kindness, respect and love we would like others to show us.

We hope you enjoy reading this book as much as we have enjoyed creating it. *Pit Road Pets* will warm your heart and soothe your soul. Consider curling up with your furry best friend to read it.

Bobby Allison
Max, Ozzie & Sandy

"**W**e had a dog, years back, named Underdog. Well, that wasn't his first name. Our son, Davey, was crazy about Red Farmer. He'd take up with him from time to time. He wanted to name that dog 'Ol' Red Farmer'. I said, 'Davey, you need to pick another name. You can't call that dog Red Farmer.' So he picked Underdog.

"Nickey was another of our dogs. He was a 'Heinz 57'. He was good with all the kids; easy to have in the house. He was very well housebroken and took good care of himself; he was a neat and clean dog.

"One day, when Davey and Clifford were in their late teens, this dog showed up at our house without a hair on its body. We took it over to the vet. He had mange, the kind people could get. Thank goodness they treated him immediately. The dog responded to the treatments and looked beautiful.

"All of our dogs seem to have had special needs. Our son-in-law, Scott, is amazing and a huge help. Our daughter Carrie makes all the dog food from scratch; that is how invested they are in their animals.

"We all feel like we have a strong appreciation for the pet world. Spaying and neutering your animals helps control the number of unwanted pets. Take home an animal if you see one that needs help. A little extra tender loving care goes a long way."

As told by Bobby Allison

"We were looking for a Cairn Terrier. One of the guys at work had Sandy and several Dobermans. He brought her to me for a little easier lifestyle. She was about six months old when we got her. Having lost my brother, Clifford, is what had me on a massive search for a dog. They are a great source of comfort.

"A lady that worked with my husband brought Ozzie into the shop when he was eight weeks old. When we saw him for the first time, he had been promised to another family. He did come back to us, though. By the time we got him, he had been to five homes in about four months' time - one home included twin babies. I took him to the training classes at PetsMart, and that's

who helped me get him straightened out. He was wild; you could tell he'd been abused. It just goes to show you the kind of results you can get with a little determination and dedication. I guess it was meant to be.

"I was looking for a Jack Russell, because we thought Sandy needed a friend; she was lonely. We would visit my in-laws frequently, and every time we'd go over to their home we would see this little black dog lying in the middle of the road. We decided that the little black dog needed a home. We said, 'What the heck?' and took him to the vet on a Friday. On Monday we got the phone call; he had a heart condition and needed open heart surgery. A few weeks later he had the surgery, and he's been good to go ever since. Max is my protector.

"They have all been such great pets. They respond to your presence. They respond to you when you call them, and when you play with them or give them a treat. I think we are very lucky to have these dogs in our lives. No matter the cost, it's worth it all."

As told by Carrie Allison Hewitt 🐾

Above: Bobby Allison pictured with wife Judy and granddogs Max, Sandy, and Ozzie

Right: Bobby Allison pictured with daughter Carrie and granddogs Max, Sandy and Ozzie

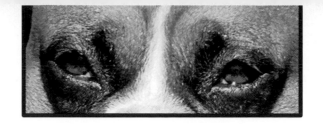

Greg Biffle
Foster & Gracie

"**I** looked for a dog for a month or two, made a lot of calls and did my research. I found Foster in Hickory, North Carolina. I wanted to get a dog from someone who wasn't just in it to make money – no puppy mills. I ended up meeting with this couple, and they had just had the one litter. That weekend would be the first available time for the puppies to actually leave their mother. I picked out Foster. It was a given; I could just see character written all over his face.

"I went out to get the car ready to take him home. I got him situated on the front seat, left the car running and ran back inside to say my goodbyes. When I came out, evidently Foster had stood on the armrest to look out the window and stepped on the lock and locked the car, with the keys in it, in less than a minute. I felt so bad; he was crying, so I called the tow truck and had the guy come 'slim-jim' the door open. Right off the bat, Foster cost me an extra fifty bucks.

"I have first child syndrome with him. He's incredible; he knows what you're saying. He's mellow and laid-back. He knows how to open and close doors at the shop; he jumps up and opens the door with his paw. He's so smart; it only takes me a few minutes to teach him a new trick.

"Gracie is Foster's daughter. We had one litter with Foster, so she's pretty special, too. I love having both of them at the track. It's a great distraction because of the stress. You never have a perfect day, and even if you do, what's tomorrow going to be like? Usually tomorrow's not going to be perfect, either – so if I'm irritated about something and I come back to the coach and see the dogs, it's awesome. He's so gentle, and Gracie is so loving. It's the love they give that can change your day.

"I'll take a shower, and Gracie is just waiting for me right there on the bath mat. We do so much together. They come with me to the race shop every day, they go in the car, they come to the property, they go to the track and they fly on the plane. I never leave the house without them. If I have to go somewhere early, Foster has to come; he's still a little clingy early in the morning. Of course, Foster and Gracie are our kids, and we treat them like they are our kids.

"I think the main problem people have with pets is not being in control. They find animals uncontrollable. Animals need space, they need to be taught and they need boundaries. They need to run and exercise. Throw the ball for them; interaction is the key. Please don't chain

up your animals; spend time with them and make them a big part of your day.

"Research your breed so you know what you're getting into. We don't like the idea of mass breeding; that's not what they're here for. People have to understand that animals have feelings just like we do, so you can't in any way mistreat them. Before you get an animal, you have to commit to spaying or neutering at a young age. Animals will breed over and over, given the opportunity; that's what the problem is. If everyone would take responsibility for their pets from the start, there wouldn't be all these shelters and unwanted animals. It is worth it. We all need to be a part of the solution and do our part." 🐾

Greg Biffle pictured with Nicole Lunders, Foster and Gracie

" *It's the love they give that can change your day.* **"**

Matt Borland
B.J., Cody, Cricket, Joe & Simba

"**S**imba was a gift to Stacy to have as a shop pet when she had her animal grooming business. B.J. is 14; he's a Shepherd-Collie mix. Cody was a wedding gift to me from Stacy; I really wanted a Malamute. He'll be six soon. Then there's Cricket – well, we call

Matt Borland pictured with wife Stacy, daughters Alli and Sami, dogs B.J., Cricket and Cody, cat Simba and parrot Joe

her Fate because she almost died as a puppy; she had pneumonia. We had her treated and brought her home. We felt like it was meant to be, hence the name Fate. Joe came into Stacy's pet shop and was the only bird that could say 'Stacy's Pets,' so he was a keeper.

"It's fun to come home to all the girls and all the animals – and we have a plenty, between home and Stacy's shop. From time to time, there'll be a new face. It's a regular petting zoo most of the time – always a random pet or two in addition to our own.

"Stacy always picks up strays. We made an agreement and a timeline, and she will always find them a good home. I think that's why she married me. Pets are a pretty big part of our world; they always have been, and I'm guessing they always will be. They make our house a home." 🐾

Jeff Burton
Clover, Hunter, Othello, Squeaky & Tiny

"**O**ur daughter, Paige, was fascinated by and very interested in horses at a very young age, but with horses you have to wait until children are five for lessons. She loved it so much that we just knew it was something she was going to stay in, so when she was seven we bought our first pony, Squeaky. Since then, we are now up to eight horses.

"These animals mean the world to our children and Kim. She dropped everything in her life to follow my career and never had time to pursue a hobby; she never had time to do anything other than what I was doing. This is the first time she's had a chance to do something for herself. I don't ride, but I like having a project going at all times. I'm the project manager. If there's a piece of equipment that needs to be purchased, that's my job, but the horses are more about Kim and Paige and in that, it's good for me because they are so happy. It's a part of who they are and who they are becoming.

"I love having Hunter around; he's so well behaved. He was perfectly trained when we got him. He was a birthday present for Paige, with the understanding that he was a family pet. It never stops – she always wants another pet. My child is an animal lover big time; she's so comfortable with them and around them, and she's learned a tremendous amount about responsibility. This summer, her job was to work at the stables; she's 10 and she did it. We're really proud of her. She enjoyed it, too.

"You really do need to respect animals. They are living creatures that do think and do have a heart and do have feelings, and if you spend any time around them you realize that. If you are a pet owner, you do have a responsibility to do it the right way. It's our responsibility to take care of them, whether it be the horse or the cat or the dog. Hold up your end of the bargain. Pay attention to them; they deserve it, they want it and they need it.

"We have 49 pets – rabbits, guinea pigs, hamsters, many, many fish, horses, frogs, cats and a dog. I expect there'll be more before I wake up tomorrow!" 🐾

"I've worked in the stables the last couple of summers. When I get to the stables, the first thing I like to do is ride. I come in from riding, give my horse a bath, and work in the stables for at least two hours cleaning, giving the horses fresh water, feeding them all and mucking the stalls. They make me really, really happy, and it makes me relax from my schoolwork. I feel like every time I ride I get better; I learn more and how to be better. I really enjoy the time my mom and I spend together, too."

—Paige Burton

Jeff Burton pictured with wife Kim, children Paige and Harrison, dog Hunter, and horses Othello, Squeaky and Tiny

66 *My brother, Harrison, really likes the guinea pigs and the rabbits and our dog, Hunter.* **99**

—*Paige Burton*

Kurt Busch
Ginger & Jim

"**I**'d grown up with West Highland Terriers all my life. Just merely because of a very hectic three years, I had been without a pet. When I was 18, my West Highland Terrier passed away. By age 21 I had things in order, so I started to look for a puppy. I finally felt like I was in a place where the racing was established enough to again have a dog in my life.

"My grandmother had a Cairn Terrier, which is what Jim is. I had about three or four years to get to know her Cairn, and the breed really appealed to me. The Cairn seemed a bit more mild-tempered and playful.

"I found Jim just cruising through a pet store. I had to have him. He had that 'puppy in the window' look – such character and personality. He was the one doing circles, which is what I do for a living; like father, like son. It is a father-son-like relationship; I treat him like a child. He needs to learn things, yet we have so much fun together.

"Jim gets to travel and see the world. I had a gas taking him out to Kansas last year because he's a 'Toto' dog. He was on TV, and I think he really liked it, too.

"When Jim was little, most of the time it was, 'Damn it, Jim!' We went to puppy school together. He's so smart. This dog really senses moods. He'll go and hide if I come in the door a bit too quickly. He always knows. He disappears for 10 to 20 minutes. I'll have to coax him out; he's really in tune with me. I'm there for him, he's there for me. He gives me space when I need it. We spend a lot of time together. He really likes going out to our land where he has room to roam. He plays with the goats, he rules the roost, and every other dog answers to him.

"I love his name; it is short and quick. He has a first and last name: Jim Busch. It just feels like he is my child, like he's human. He gives you that sense of love and caring. When we travel together, we have fun as if we're sharing experiences to make the time pass easier. Animals are so like children; you have to give them time to learn, to play and of course obedience, that they must learn as well. I think a smart, well-mannered dog is more appreciative in his own life. They are well behaved when people come to visit, so people tend to respond in a more positive way. You can just see the connection the owner and the pet have that way.

"Eva and I decided to get Jim a little sister. We got Ginger. She loves and adores Jim and

follows him everywhere. She is just always right there, playful and happy. She's a little cuddler, too. Jim gets too hot, but Ginger will sleep with us at all times. They give us a feeling of family, closeness. It is tough right now to consider the responsibility of human children, but it's a nice bridge to seeing Eva's motherhood, my fatherhood, and the channels we have to take as far as the proper steps are concerned. We love Jim and Ginger so much that it is part of our daily routine to think about how we are going to take care of them."

Kurt Busch pictured with Eva and dogs Jim and Ginger

"They give us a feeling of family, closeness."

Kyle Busch
Kelly & Suzie

"**K**elly was the first. I started looking for a dog around Christmas. I happened to mention it to my parents and they got all spun out about it, simply because I travel so much. At the time, I was living in Las Vegas but getting ready to make a move to North Carolina. I think they thought the timing was bad, that's all. She was such a great puppy; needless to say, here she is.

"We needed a playmate for Kelly, a sister. We found Suzie in Hickory, North Carolina. She started out very quiet, but now she's very, very loud – she is the loud one.

"It is so nice to come back to your motorcoach, if you're struggling through your weekend, and the minute that door opens you kind of get back to your life, your reality. We just relax and the two of us play and wrestle with the two of them. They are so fun-loving.

"The Busch family has always had dogs. My brother Kurt and my dad had Westies, Scotties, Yorkshire Terriers and Cairn Terriers. We are big into the Terrier family.

"A lot of the drivers, especially the younger drivers, have dogs and cats; they are like our children because we don't have any yet. You have to figure out on your own, unlike children, what their needs are, so it's huge. You must have a good connection so you can anticipate their needs before it even happens. I think the main thing my animals have taught me is respect, being as though animals don't always get a lot of that through humans as far as adopting or rescuing is concerned. Most of those animals have been abused one way or another. To respect an animal gives you the ability to respect other people out there who do dedicate their lives to bettering animals' well-being.

"We have a rescue, Lowee. We don't know what she is, how old she is or where she originally came from. She was a stray that I found. She's been through a lot. She's timid and shy, but she is so loving. Lowee was nothing but skin and bones when I found her. I was doing a photo shoot at Lowe's Motor Speedway and I saw her up against the fence. I brought her down to where we were and put her in my truck. I fed her leftover biscuits from breakfast. It looked like she hadn't eaten in months, and the rest is history. She became mine. I took her to the vet and got her all taken

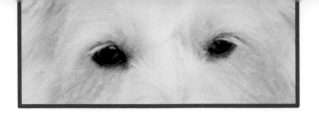

care of and cleaned up; she was so appreciative, you could tell. My grandmother fell in love with her, so Lowee is hers now. She just wants to be loved and she is, for sure.

"I personally think everyone should love animals. They are there for companionship; they are man's best friend. Try to do your best – whatever it takes – to be good to them. We know what the ultimate prize is." 🐾

Kyle Busch pictured with Erica Dewey
and dogs Kelly and Suzie

Larry Carter
Maggie

"The story about Maggie is an interesting one. I was working with an up-and-coming driver, Stuart Kirby, and we were testing a Busch car in Kentucky. Stuart had a friend that had been in a very serious automobile accident and was paralyzed from the waist down. His friend came driving up in his van and there was Maggie, hanging out the window. We started talking, and he explained to me that he was having a very difficult time taking care of himself, let alone the poor dog. She wasn't getting what she needed from him, and he really wanted to find a good home for her.

"My son was six at the time, and I knew he'd love her. I decided to take her; I felt like it was meant to happen that way. The airline let me put her under the seat, and home she went!

"I knew my son was really ready for a dog, but I wasn't sure about my wife, so I just didn't say anything. Well, it turned out the way I thought it would, thank goodness — they both loved her.

"She is such a good dog, no trouble at all. She's so smart and so protective of my son. I guess things like this are just meant to be. I couldn't have asked for a better buddy for my son.

"I was raised with dogs. We always had plenty around the house, so I've always enjoyed them. I work around cars all the time, and I bet these guys at the shop can tell you what car they were driving at 16. I can do that, but with dogs. I can tell you what dog I had when I was six years old more readily than what car I had when I was 20 years old.

"The worst thing we are dealing with in our society, as far as animals are concerned, is the overpopulation. We can't take care of all of them. We got Maggie spayed early; we did not want the burden of puppies or to impose that on anyone else. We want the dog that we do have to be loved and well cared for.

"I would encourage people to add a pet to their lives because it is such a great addition to the family unit. It keeps and brings people together and is a great common bond. At the same time, you've got to be realistic; they are a responsibility. Please, at least help an animal in need. Make a donation or do volunteer work. Help us all make an animal's life better." 🐾

Stacy Compton

Billie, Ginger, Miss Daisy, Miss Kitty, Tom, pheasants, quail, geese, ducks, cattle, a llama & a miniature donkey

"**M**iss Kitty was the first of our bunch of animals; she came from my first house. She was a junkyard cat. We rescued nine kittens and didn't know what happened to the mother cat. Miss Kitty was the runt of the litter; she was very small, but she stuck with us.

"We've had as many as 17 cats at one time. We have a cat house out back. It's heated for the winter and we've got fans for the summer. From the old house we brought all 17 cats, originally. We did all the things they tell you to do when relocating cats. We moved them in crates and at night, but 15 of them still went back to the old house, which is about 10 miles from the new house. It took 17 days for all of them to finally get back to the old house. Miss Kitty and Tom, her son, were the two that never left. Miss Kitty turned out to be the best indoor cat. We love her so much.

"One day Ginger came home with Vickie. Surprise! She had wanted a chocolate Lab for a long time and finally found one. Vickie didn't want to leave her outside, so during the training process we made a home for her in the garage. Well, she wanted to be with us so much that she dug into the wall and almost all the way into the dining room! It's all okay now. Ginger has a best friend that distracts her from any potential dry wall destruction: Billie, the Billy Goat. They are inseparable. Billie just showed up one day, and not a moment too soon. She's been the perfect playmate for Ginger ever since.

"We got Miss Daisy at the track from a friend. We snagged her up immediately. Before our daughter Olivia was born, Daisy would go everywhere with me; she still does. Whether it's the Gator or the tractor, she just wants to be with me 24/7. Getting her was the best thing we have ever done. It's such a blessing to be loved like that. Wow, when Olivia is old enough to realize it, we'll have a petting zoo.

"Our entire family has always been animal lovers. Although I've always had cats, I really am allergic, but I don't care; I just keep the cabinets well stocked with Benadryl. People know we love cats and sometimes they just drop them off on our property. We will spay and neuter them and help find good homes for them. We have always adopted and rescued. Most of the time, those animals make better pets.

"We like to be an active part of our environment. We've gotten involved with a state program, like what Ward Burton is doing with his wildlife foundation. We've been involved for

Stacy Compton pictured with wife Vickie, daughter Olivia, Miss Kitty (cat), Ginger (Lab), Billie (Billy Goat), Miss Daisy (Shi Tzu), and a newly-hatched quail (right)

about six or seven years now. We help restore the wetlands and the woods for the area ducks and geese. We've also planted food plots all over our farm. We're trying to get the deer population where it needs to be by supplying them with the proper proteins. This year we released 2,000 quail and probably 10 sets of pheasants. We have a quail farm where we collect the eggs, help them through the incubation process and take care of them until they are ready to be released back into the wild.

"It is our future, and especially that of my child, that I am the most concerned with. I want her to appreciate the very things my parents taught me to appreciate. Animals are the best things that can ever happen to people. Look at all the good things that come along as a result of them. Life in any form is so precious. Aren't we the lucky ones?" 🐾

> 66*They are inseparable. Billie just showed up one day, and not a moment too soon. She's been the perfect playmate for Ginger ever since.*99

Bill & Gail Davis
Vegas

"**O**ur story begins long ago. We had a mixed breed; I call them 'All American Dogs'. Her name was Kitti, and she was extremely dear to us. She weighed about 90 pounds. We were crazy about her. After she died, we kept thinking another dog would

come into our lives, but it didn't. We happened to go to a dinner party in Hickory, North Carolina, one night, and our host and hostess had a Briard kennel. After dinner, I asked if we could see the dogs. All of a sudden this big, beautiful dog came in and laid down on me.

"Bill secretively called our friend, Merry Jeanne Millner, who hosted us on that fateful night, and told her he wanted to surprise me with a dog. At Christmas he gave me two 8"x10" photographs of the puppy, not yet ready to come home. Vegas was born December 19, 2004.

"We picked her up in Phoenix, Arizona, in March on the way to Las Vegas – thus came the name Vegas. We call her 'Little Miss Las Vegas' because she is very showy. She is my life. Although Bill and I have always worked, I get up every morning and onto the grooming table she goes. She is definitely my new hobby. She's a Mama's girl!

"The last year has been fabulous since we've had her. I just think pets enhance the quality of your life tremendously. People who don't have pets are really missing out on one of the greatest loves. It is a sacrifice. You have to think of them

first, but the rewards are so great.

"We've had dogs and cats all our lives, and Vegas has made a huge difference in our lives. My pets have been my children. I tell Vegas 20 times a day that I love her.

"It tears me up to see dogs chained and tied up. You are the center of their life, and they want to be with you. If you're going to commit, fully commit. We are all extremely distressed by the number of pets that are euthanized. It is also imperative to understand the importance of spaying and neutering. Thousands of animals are euthanized in the state of North Carolina alone. We have to get the message out. It's our responsibility to educate our children."

As told by Gail Davis 🐾

Bill and Gail Davis with Vegas

Dale Earnhardt, Jr.
Killer

"I had been looking for a dog, and my sister knew that Greg Biffle's dog, Foster, had just had a litter. She saw Killer, brought him over to me and that was it; I took him home that weekend. It was great.

"I hadn't had a dog since I was a little kid, so when I got to the point where I thought I could handle one, I had to go over all the details. You've got to be ready for the responsibility of taking care of them and giving them a home. When they look at you and they want something, you've got to know what they want and what's going on with them.

"I don't have a lot of experience with training dogs and getting them in a routine, but it's been real easy with Killer. Our personalities are really the same. We're real laid-back; we like to sleep and lay around. He fits in perfectly because he's not real hyper, and we're on the same page pretty much all the time. He's kind of a reason to be happy, especially if you've had a bad day or if you get kind of selfish and start feeling like, 'I didn't get what I wanted out of the day.' It's just like how your friends cheer you up; your dog can, too. It's a good reality check that there are more important things going on in the world than what you are trying to achieve that day, that moment.

"Killer has such a distinct personality. It's simply the little things he does that make me laugh, like when he paws at the door, and the look on his face when he figures things out on his own. Sometimes I challenge him. I love to watch his process. You can just see him thinking and trying to figure it out. Most often you get to where you both understand what he wants or what he's trying to do. That's the fun and the satisfaction right there. He also has great manners.

"If I could take NASCAR fans to a shelter and show them what it's like for animals, it would make a big difference. Some friends brought me to a shelter, and that was eye-opening enough for me. I was shocked at what the shelter employees explained to me about the weekly transition and turnover of animals. You wouldn't believe the number of dogs and cats that go in and out. Obviously more go in than get adopted out.

"I was amazed at how nice the animals were. When you think of a shelter, you think of an old, scraggly, jail-like facility. But there were some sweet, nice animals there. Obviously, right then and there, you want to take them all home. If you get a chance to see what the system is like and realize the hard work that goes into these shelters, it is enough to understand the problem. I suggest checking out the shelters when you're looking for a pet. And make sure to spay and neuter; it's good insurance!" 🐾

> **"** *He's got great manners.* **"**

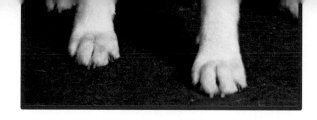

Carl Edwards
Shelter Dog, Lucky

"Our family always had dogs while we were growing up. I especially remember our German Shepherds. For as long as I can remember, my dad had them at the shop. We had a great dog, Bear, that just passed away; I think he was about 14.

"To me, dogs have always been so awesome, always happy and always eager to play. I think animals are so loving, no matter what. Companionship with a dog is so personal, so unique.

"We had a dog named Dusty. This dog was hilarious; her eyes went in different directions. We were always entertained by that and her personality. Trust me, I've had a lot of great relationships and good laughs with dogs, no matter where they come from.

"It is so important to spay and neuter, because there is nothing sadder than seeing an animal without a home. Have respect for a life and the quality of life. Feed them, groom them and, most of all, make sure they have their freedom – a good fenced-in yard for exercise. It's always been important to me, and I always made sure my animals got properly exercised. I see a lot more animals in my future, and maybe a house with some land and a great backyard where my future pets can catch Frisbees and wrestle. They really do add an element to your life like no other." 🐾

Carl Edwards pictured with Lucky, a shelter dog from the Humane Society of Concord & Greater Cabarrus County in Concord, North Carolina (www.dogsaver.org/cabarrushumane)

Ray Evernham
Lizzie & Schecky

"**S**checky is almost 12. We had an associate sponsorship with Kal Kan, now called Pedigree, on the DuPont Chevrolet. At the time, Mike Murphy, who was president, took Jeff Gordon and me out to dinner. He offered us all the dog food you could ever need, so I piped up and said, 'I don't have a dog.' Mike spoke up and said, 'I'll send you one.' And a month later we had Schecky. He's been a big part of our family ever since.

"Schecky is such a great guy dog; we have such a good relationship. We walk down to the lake together. I used to take him in the Durango a lot, but he's older now and his legs don't work as well as they used to. But, no matter the day, the mood, if we win or lose, life is good for Schecky and me.

"Everybody in the neighborhood knows Schecky. He didn't do so well with the invisible fence so we have an iron fence now. He was a visitor to just about everybody's home within a few square miles. People used to call me up and say, 'Hey, Ray, Schecky's over here. He's lying down, just hanging out right now. He's fine, don't worry about him.' He's kind of an escape artist, a social butterfly of sorts. He just loves people, loves, loves, *loves* people, and people love Schecky.

"Ray J, my son, also wanted a small dog, so my wife Mary, Ray J and I decided on a Shi Tzu. We got Lizzie; Ray J named her after Lizzie McGuire. Lizzie is the princess of the house; she's a high-maintenance girl. As long as I give her a treat she's my friend, and if I don't she ignores me. She can be bought. She'll sleep with Ray J until she knows he's asleep, then she makes her move. They all love you the same no matter what's going on. You know no matter what at least somebody is going to be happy to see you.

"We lead a hectic life and many of us have animals on the road. Sometimes they are the only person…Did I say person? Well, they are people. Anyway, they are the only ones to talk to. I am a grown man and I still talk to Schecky like a kid. My neighbors must think I'm crazy; I'll have full-on conversations about the day with him.

"It doesn't take much to rescue an animal. I applaud all who do and all who work for the cause. Hopefully we can get the message out that we need to embrace our animal community. Just look at how much Schecky and Lizzie do for us. Look at those faces!"

Ray Evernham pictured with wife Mary, son Ray J, Schecky and Lizzie

Bobby Hamilton, Jr.
Coco

"**I** wanted a Bulldog and Stephanie wanted a Yorkie. We knew Terry Labonte had a little Yorkie, so we went over to see it. Once I held it, I knew that's what we needed.

"We went to see the breeder, and she really drilled us. She wanted to know if we had kids, if we were home a lot, what I did for a living, where I lived. Well, I guess we answered all the questions right, because she pointed to a basket and there was this itty-bitty black dot. We picked her up and we've had her ever since.

"She's daddy's little girl, for sure. When we got her, she was really Stephanie's dog. She was going to walk Coco and feed her and take her out at night. Well, that lasted about a week. I did it all; the housebreaking, the taking her out at night. I think it shows because we're so bonded. Wherever I go, she wants to go, too. Even at night she'll start out sleeping on Stephanie's side, but before the night is over she's back over with me.

"No matter how bad the day, win, lose or draw, she doesn't care. She doesn't care if there's a paycheck. She doesn't care if there's food in the refrigerator. As long as she can see you, it's all she cares about, along with getting up in your lap the minute you walk in. Even before Hailey was born, the minute you walked in your mind was off your job.

"She's just herself. She's got her own little personality; like a person with lots of hair. She listens. She wears her feelings on her shoulder; if you catch on to her, you can see it in her ears and her tail. She's her own little person.

"I've had some dogs that are dumb as rocks. I mean, we loved them just the same, but Coco is really smart. We treat her just like a kid. We even send her to daycare; she needs that companionship.

"We had a unique pet growing up, Mr. Sparkles. My dad had a pilot back then named Jerry, and he happened to be a big fisherman – a real wildlife kind of guy. He was out on the lake one day and heard a ruckus coming through the trees; here comes a deer being chased by a big cat, and behind him was a little deer. The baby deer missed the turn and ran right into the water. Jerry scooped him right up and brought him to my dad. Jerry didn't know what to do with the thing, so my dad said, 'We'll take him.' They say not to pin them in all the way, so we built a big old pen with a big opening, and we even had dogs everywhere. My mom named him Mr. Sparkles because he had white star-like markings on his back. He was so at home with us. One day I was playing a computer game and I felt like someone was watching me; I'd look around and nothing.

I'd look around some more, still nothing. Finally I looked down, and there was Mr. Sparkles curled up in a ball on the floor – rack and all – staring up at me. You'd look up and there he'd be in the living room, just hanging out. He would come in and eat off the counter; he'd watch TV. We ended up giving him to a no-kill park; he just got too big. We can still track him and know where he is and visit him if we want.

"I'd also like to add something about treating your pets well. You see a lot of pets chained up outside on hot days with a dirty pan of water, or pets left alone in cars with the windows up on hot days. Think of the extra heat with all that hair. Can you only imagine how hot they must be? Treat them the way you would want to be treated. You go out there, chain yourself up, live in a wood box and drink dirty water and see how you like it. Or go to Kroger, roll up your window and turn off the car and sit there in the heat. Put yourself in the position of the dog. Just treat them the way you want to be treated." 🐾

❝As long as she can see you, it's all she cares about, along with getting up in your lap the minute you walk in.❞

Bobby Hamilton, Jr. pictured with wife Stephanie, daughter Hailey and dog Coco

Kevin Harvick
bebe, Endy, Liza, Lo & Sebastian

"**W**e went over to Judy and Richard Childress' for a visit. They had just gotten their fully trained German Shepherd, and it just so happened that there were puppies there as well. So, needless to say, we went home with a puppy of our own; funny how that works. Our first puppy was 'bebe'. She's the cat chaser. Oh, she loves to give them a good chasing; we think she lives for it!

"Endy is fully trained in protection and obedience; he's the king of the house. We wanted our male German Shepherd to be the biggest and meanest he could be, and an awesome companion; he's all that and more. Endy is very dependent upon DeLana, very. I think you call that the ultimate bond.

"Then there's Lo; we got her in Dallas, Texas. We'd never had a little dog, but really she rules the whole bunch; she's got a big personality for a small dog. Lo goes with us to the track. She's very mobile being the size she is; she travels well and enjoys it. She loves Endy and mostly sleeps alongside him; now that's a sight.

"We have a few cats – Sebastian and Liza. They, for the most part, do their own thing; dodging the dogs and trying to typically remain independent. We adopted Liza from a PetsMart. She's not into crowds at all. Sebastian was adopted too. He's a clever one.

"We definitely have a few of each of these guys, and we love them all so much. We've always had dogs, so that's what we're really used to. But cats are low maintenance; they've wound up being very cool.

"They think we've hung the moon. Even if they're in trouble and they give you that little look, it's all over. Some days you're just so tired, but you know you're going to feed them, you know you're going to play with them and you know that they depend on you. It makes us feel good that they rely on us. For us, they give so much.

"If we could take every animal home from a shelter, we would. I know that it's not possible, but at least our area is doing the right thing to help in this crusade. We just want everyone everywhere to help out and hopefully one day this problem of overpopulation won't exist. We think there is a home for all animals, and we are grateful just to know that we can help in our own small way to raise awareness. Thank goodness for the people that run the shelters and for those who adopt."

> **❝** *It makes us feel good that they rely on us. For us, they give so much.***❞**

Kevin Harvick pictured with wife DeLana,
dogs bebe, Lo and Endy, and cat Liza

Dale Jarrett
Samantha & Zoe

"Zoe was a gift from Kelley's brother, Kevin; he's a big animal lover. We knew when we moved into this house we had room for an animal, so for Christmas, Uncle Kevin came with a surprise bundle for us. She was a beautiful Lab puppy. What a joy for the kids; Christmas and a new puppy! She's been a big part of the family ever since. Now she's all grown up at seven years old.

"Samantha came from right here in Hickory, North Carolina. I was in the mall with my family and we decided to visit the pet store. We'd been looking for a cat because the one we had ran away. Kelley grew up with Siamese cats, so it seemed like a natural fit when we saw the Siamese kittens. I told the girls we'd think about it, but just as they all walked out I walked back in and bought Samantha. She hollered and screamed all the way home, and that hasn't stopped since 1993; she's very vocal, very!

"When Zack and I are playing ball or we're up at the batting cage, Zoe goes with us. She knows that's her time to run and get exercise, too. She knows she can count on us for that.

"I'll never forget one time when Zoe was about a year-and-a-half old. Kelley had been shopping in Indy the weekend before and bought me some shoes and things for the house, some really nice stuff. She and the kids were taking off for the beach the next week, and she reminded me that the UPS guys would be delivering. So, I put a note on the door as to where the driver should leave everything. Somehow that sign came down. I was out playing golf with my brother, and when I came home that evening I stopped at the top of the hill to get the mail. The lights came on, and it looked like a lot of things were strewn all over the yard. Yes, Zoe had had a Christmas of her own; four large boxes had been sent, and four large boxes had been opened. It was like a two-year-old on Christmas morning. Every item was examined, every item played with – shoes, lamps and clothing everywhere. She did one heck of a job opening every one of them. I guess it wasn't funny at the time, but we can look back and laugh now.

"These animals are an extension of what your family is. They factor into everything you do. It makes you think about others in a little better light. If you take care of your animals, clearly you'll take better care of your children. It's a great lesson for kids; I know it was for me

growing up. I had to be fully responsible for feeding and watering my dog. It is a great life lesson. You can't get a friend more loyal than your dog.

"If people would just look at the opportunity to get a pet, there are great opportunities out there for them at the shelters. We need to take care of the ones we have here and now."

Dale Jarrett pictured with wife Kelley, son Zachary, daughters Karsyn and Natalee, dog Zoe and cat Samantha

Jason Jarrett
Poseidon & Steele

"**C**hristina and I had gone to a flea market and came across this batch of puppies. We played with them, walked around a little more and talked about them. Fast forward to later that night. We were back at home, and Christina said that she had to go out for an errand. I didn't question where she was going, but I suspected what she was up to, though. Sure enough, she came home with Steele. Evidently, Christina had gotten the owner's contact information at the flea market and had gone to their home that night and picked out Steele. Honestly, she wanted him so badly that she used her car payment to buy him.

"I had always said that I wouldn't have a dog at that point in my life; it's a distraction. I made many excuses, but after the first night, even with his little 'accident' in our bed – he'd been wormed that day and, well, the rest is history – I loved him just the same. This dog changed my mind in less than one night, and I guess you would say that was a big bonding experience for me.

"When Steele was about two, our neighbors had another Siberian Husky just like him. They just couldn't handle him, and they were ready to turn him over to the shelter. Christina and I intervened and adopted Poseidon. We thought it was a good fit, and that way Steele could have a buddy.

"These animals have taught me a lot about love. I'm the guy that didn't want dogs – too much responsibility. It gives you somebody other than yourself to think about. Obviously, you care that way about your significant other, but to extend that to an animal is most definitely love – just a very different and unique kind of love because you have to; you must take care of them. They need attention. I never thought I would care this much about these dogs as I do, until they were ours. It is a lifestyle change, and you have to be ready for it. There is a payoff for sure.

"Be prepared to take care of the animals you have. It is expensive, but with that comes the peace of mind that you have done the right thing by your animal. By getting our animals fixed, we have relieved ourselves of any further burden. They deserve every bit the same standard of living that you have; without spaying and neutering, they will not have that. These two dogs are good for each other, and even better for us." 🐾

Jimmie Johnson
Maya & Roxanne ("Roxie")

"**W**e had friends that had put down a deposit on Roxie but found another dog they wanted in the process. Well, they knew who to call; we immediately went and looked at her. The minute we walked in, I knew we'd be walking out with her. 'We'll take her,'

with no hesitation. We knew she would be a great pup.

"We got Maya shortly after. We put Roxie and Maya together to see how they would get along, and they played really well. They are such wonderful companions for us. They go to all the races; really, they go everywhere. Depending on where it is, it could be in a carrier or in Chandra's purse. They go shopping; they go to restaurants, on planes, helicopters, boats. I must say, they have the life.

"They are so laid-back that it really does help calm things down sometimes. They create such a nice distraction from other things that are going on in our busy lives. Next thing you know, I'm up off the floor with a big smile on my face and all is right with the world.

"The fact that they are like children to us makes the relationship very special, because they do so much with us and our other family members. It makes them even more like kids.

"If you commit to an animal, make sure you commit to the time and the love they need. We think that Maya may have had a bad experience, so we just keep showering her with love. The more we do, the more she comes around. It takes time and energy, but the outcome is the reward. She is a different dog today than when we got her. Just fill them with love.

"They walked down the aisle at our wedding. We got a lot of feedback from it, too. So many people thought it was corny, but they were the talk of the celebration. They share in our love. They stole the show. We just love them so much that not seeing to their needs isn't a thought or an option.

"We made sure right away that both girls were spayed. We didn't plan on breeding them, but if there were an accident, what would we do? We never took the risk; we addressed the responsibility right away. Animals have brains and hearts, and they feel and love and have the same instincts we do. You must honor that."

Jimmie Johnson pictured with wife Chandra and dogs Roxanne "Roxie" and Maya

"I must say,
they have the life."

Junior Johnson
Doodles, Princess, Spud & The Colonel

"**F**riends of ours had a litter of puppies, and that's where we got Spud. My intent was to try and make him a working dog to help with the cattle and all, but he got to be such a pet, he wound up just being a pet. He made every bit as good a pet as he would have a cow dog, so it all worked out.

"Gypsy was a Chesapeake Bay Retriever. I made a present of her for Lisa. She had been wanting a puppy, so I put Gypsy behind the sofa and waited for Lisa to come home from work. It was a grand surprise, and she was the most incredible dog. It was a very sad day when she got run over by a car; she survived it, but she started having seizures. She was so smart and talented and the most devoted dog you've ever seen. She was kind of like a guard dog when the kids came along. She wouldn't let anyone between them, and if you tried she'd bite you. We were so fond of her, especially because she looked after them; we never had to worry when they were out playing.

"We got Princess shortly after Gypsy passed away. She took up with me. She rides with me a lot on the farm. She has become devoted; I'm sure it's because we do spend a lot of time together. Then we got Doodles. She is basically the kids' dog now – it's like three kids out there playing. Both Doodles and Princess are such water dogs;

they'll go swimming with the kids, and you'll look out the window and you'll see four heads bobbing in the pool. Doodles is real protective, too. At night she will get her bone and all Lisa has to say is, 'Doodles, go sleep with Robert,' and it's good night.

"A dog is a lot of company. If they like you, they're always there for you and they don't talk back! Animals need discipline, but they don't know what you want them to do. You'll have to teach them – and when you get done teaching them, you'll never know a more devoted companion. I for one don't ever want to witness mistreatment of an animal, ever. Teaching them is the key. If you develop a close relationship, they understand and pick up on your nonverbal signals; therefore, you take the time to nurture that relationship. It just takes time and patience, and what a reward in the end.

"Lisa and I are both so fond of all the animals we have had and do have in our lives. Lisa just rescued one of the displaced dogs from Hurricane Katrina as a gift for her mother. Twenty-four hours was all it took for that very grateful little

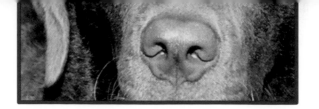

dog to adapt to someone loving her and giving her a home. They've adapted to one another like ducks to water. It's such a great situation for both of them, and in this case it didn't take much. It's worth the investment of a little time and a little love. If you try adopting, it could change your life in 24 hours for the better."

Junior Johnson pictured with wife Lisa, son Robert, daughter Meredith, dogs Doodles, Princess (above), and Spud, and horse The Colonel

Kasey Kahne
Kalvin

"Growing up, we had cats, Dobermans and Rottweilers. The Doberman, Hooker, was a great dog. He was a great guard dog, too, but he was really sweet. If you didn't know him, he could keep you sitting in your car, staring you down; let's just say that

can be pretty intimidating. Those who knew him could just jump right out of the car and everything would be fine.

"I'm a dog guy. After we lost Hooker, we got two Rottweilers. They were big, sweet babies, such good dogs. Our dogs were indoor and outdoor dogs. They loved coming inside with us, just hanging out and watching TV. You could see the love in their faces and the appreciation to be with all of us.

"Kalvin is a rescue. He belongs to my sister Shannon and brother-in-law Jarrod. He was found roaming the streets of Charlotte. They think he was used as bait in dog fights because of all the scarring up and down his legs and chest, and his tongue has a piece missing out of it. They think he was used as bait for Pit Bulls; I cannot even imagine that. Kalvin has been an awesome dog, a great dog for all of us. He's been like a family dog.

"The Boxer rescue is a wonderful organization, so people should check these rescue sites out first. Don't waste a lot of money when

there are all these dogs out there that need a good home; give them a chance.

"The main reason I don't have a dog right now is because I don't feel like I have enough time to give to a deserving dog. Definitely, when I'm in a more settled place, I will get one. I'd love to have a dog right now if everything was right. Don't get an animal if you can't take care of it; wait. You've got to be fair. You've got to be ready. Don't jump into anything until you're ready." 🐾

Matt Kenseth
Charlotte & Lars

"**I** surprised Katie with Lars. I went and got him at a veterinary clinic in Statesville, North Carolina. I told her we could not have an indoor cat, and then I secretively went out and got her Lars. There were a bunch of kittens that someone had just dropped off, so I rescued him.

"Lars was our only cat for a while and I thought, 'We go out of town so much, and he sits home alone. He's got to be bored. We've got to get him a pal.' So we started looking for a second cat. We heard that a vet in Denver, North Carolina, just down the road, had some homeless cats. We went to see them, and we brought home Charlotte.

"These two cats are like our kids in a way. It's a joy coming home, because they're always your buddy. They like to sit by us and cuddle with us when we watch TV. Lars is so entertaining. If I'm having a bad day, he'll come over and sit by me; then we'll start to wrestle, and that makes me feel better. It definitely helps along the day.

"Charlotte is different; she's so loving and thoughtful. Charlotte was an outdoor street cat. She loves having a house now and never tries to sneak out; she's so grateful. Lars, on the other hand, is just plain naughty; he tries to sneak out at any given opportunity! We came home once and couldn't find Lars; we called him and called him. I went down to the basement to do more searching; nothing. I thought I would give it a little time and sat down at my desk to do some work. All of a sudden, the ceiling tiles above my desk started moving; he was in the ceiling! He had pushed a ceiling tile up by jumping from the staircase onto a window treatment. Can you believe it? One time we came home and he had broken a leg from trying the same stunt. He's a daredevil like his father.

"They show their appreciation by eating and eating and filling up the litter box, that's for sure. The bottom line is, with life, people and animals, it's the golden rule every time. It's important to consider adoption, and more important to spay and neuter. Look at the rewards. It's good material and good laughs!" 🐾

"These two cats are like our kids in a way. It's a joy coming home, because they're always your buddy."

Matt Kenseth pictured with wife
Katie and cats Lars and Charlotte

Chad Knaus
Shelter Dog, Rusty

"**I**'ve had a lot of great pets over the years, dogs and cats. I've had an Irish Setter, a German Shepherd, a Chow Chow, a Boxer and a Bengal cat.

"Gavin, my Boxer, was my soul mate; we did everything together. Whether I was running or riding my bicycle, he would come along with me. We used to go out to this great church in Hickory, North Carolina, and play catch. We just had so much fun. I miss him, as I do all the others.

"Over my lifetime, I think these animals have taught me patience. I have 85 people who work for me, so I think the level of patience and responsibility you need clearly has some bearing on your past experiences. Animals are truly a large part of that. They teach you how to be tolerant, how to work through a system. You have to give people, like animals, an opportunity to get adjusted, time to get used to what's going on around them.

"Don't treat animals any different than you would a human being, just like any other living creature. There are so many great animals out there in the shelters to be had. So many people want the purebred dogs, but give the shelter dogs or cats a chance. There are so many cool ones out there ready for a loving home. It's not about what kind of dog it is, it's about the connection, which you can see right away!" 🐾

It's not about what kind of dog it is, it's about the connection, which you can see right away!

Chad Knaus pictured with Rusty, a shelter dog from the Iredell County Humane Society in Statesville, North Carolina (www.iredellhumane.org)

Travis Kvapil
Shelter Dogs
Bart, Libby & Socks

"**I** am from a very rural area in southern Wisconsin, and we had lots of dogs growing up. It was real country living, and we were outside a lot. It seemed that we had a lot of Cocker Spaniels. Abbey was one of the Cockers that I was especially close to. We had her when I was in middle school and high school; she was so fun and a great house dog.

"Animals are so sweet and so innocent; they're very childlike. It's fun to see their playfulness. It makes me feel good to take care of them. They're little people.

"Our family is in the process of rescuing a pup, a new addition to our family. I want this new addition to teach my kids about responsibility and the importance of taking care of something that depends on you. To have this animal, this pet that will be there for them when they get home from school or from a friend's house… I think it will bring a lot of joy, comfort and a unique bond for my children.

"Sure, you can go to breeders, but there are dogs and cats out there that need a good home. That's what we're going to do, and that is what, as a family, we encourage everyone looking for a new family member to do. I personally think it's the right thing to do, so pass it on: rescue and save a pet's life." 🐾

Travis Kvapil pictured with wife Jennifer, son Carson, daughter Kelsey and puppies from the Humane Society of Catawba County in Hickory, North Carolina (www.catawbahumanc.org). These puppies were fostered by Ryan and Krissie Newman, who adopted Socks as an addition to their own family.

66*I love that they can all go outside and entertain each other.*99

Bobby Labonte
Shelter Dog, Paco

"The biggest thing about having dogs is providing my kids with that friendship. I love that they can all go outside and entertain each other. Kids could sit inside all day if there's nothing to go outside for; that's the main reason our dogs tie our family together.

"I love when Missy and Zoe meet me at the driveway. We decided on Miniature Collies because they are a good size and very smart. The kids were small at the time, and that way they wouldn't be overwhelmed by their size; it was all manageable.

"A long time ago, my brother Terry and I found an English Setter behind a hotel in Shreveport, Louisiana. It was around 1977. We asked our dad if we could keep him, and he said that if he was there when we came back, it would be okay. We got back that night, and sure enough, he was still there. His poor teeth had been ground all the way down to nothing; this guy had been eating whatever he could find, including the can, for a very long time it appeared. We named him Fofo because of Terry's car number, 44. Home he came with us, and home he stayed for a very long time. He was the coolest dog.

"We had Fofo, a smaller dog and a duck. They all stayed in the backyard. There were two dog houses; the small one was for the duck, and Fofo and the smaller dog had the large one. Well, the duck took over the large dog house – so this big English Setter and the small dog slept in the small duck house, and the duck slept in the large dog house. The duck was real bossy.

"One day I saw Fofo out the window. He was minding his own business sunbathing in the yard, and the duck started pecking at his private parts. Talk about making a dog mad! That duck had taken over Fofo's house and ate all Fofo's food, and now he's really going to get it. The next thing I knew, Fofo had that duck by the neck and was taking him to the cleaners. I screamed out the window, 'Hey!' – and Fofo dropped the duck and all was well. He was such a great dog, and we just happened to find him.

"Animals should never, ever be abused. They have memories and feelings. If you can't tend to them, make every effort to find them a good, loving home. If you have an animal, handle that animal; if you can't handle one, don't have one – don't go there.

"We've got two bunny rabbits. Yes, two. My wife went out to get one for one of our children, and when she came home she said, 'Have you seen the bunnies?' I said, 'Bunnies, plural?' She

said, 'I felt sorry for this one because he's blind in one eye.' Marshmallow needed a pal, so Floppy came home, too.

"Animals are always a welcome addition to our family – more character, more fun!

If you have your heart set on one kind of animal, you may not find it at the shelter – but of all the animals we've had, the best ones we've gotten were adopted or rescued. I think personally we've had more luck with the rescue dogs than we have with the breeder's dogs, so I encourage everyone who may be ready to just do it and check out your shelter." 🐾

Bobby Labonte pictured with Paco, a shelter dog from the Humane Society of Catawba County in Hickory, North Carolina (www. catawbahumane.org)

66Home he came with us, and home he stayed for a very long time. He was the coolest dog.99

Claire B. Lang
Rosie

"We found Rosie through friends. Mike brought her home in a box. When he went to pick her out, he asked the girl what this one puppy's name was and she said, 'Rosie.' Mike kept watching her and she kept watching him; he knew we had to have her.

"Rosie is a hunting dog, but she is so sweet. After a stressful day she is just so sweet; she requires nothing but to love her and a little play time. She is so much fun!

"She goes hunting a lot with Mike, but sometimes she'll just lay down next to us at the end of the day when everything calms down. She does love a Frisbee; she'll circle around and around and catch it every single time. Sometimes we throw and throw. I love it because it's predictable, uncomplicated and soothing.

"We almost lost her. She got hit by a car. The vet said to put her down, but we got a second opinion and that vet said she could be saved. In conversation with the second vet, he did tell us that her pelvis and birth canal were crushed. Mike's dad told him years ago that when a dog wags his tail, it means they don't have spinal cord injuries. If she hadn't wagged her tail then, there would be no telling what would have happened. We were convinced that we could see her through and she would survive. Rosie didn't lose her leg like the fist vet expected, but she's got a little scar

on her face. She's fine; we call her Scarface. Thank goodness she's still here – we love her so much.

"When we lost our last dog, our lives were so busy that I didn't realize until she was gone how much we missed her. I think we appreciate Rosie that much more now. We could have the worst day, and she's right there for you. The joy a pet can bring to you is life-altering. Pets are great for children and adults. A dog or a cat can take you to that place where you're not thinking about anything. How great is that?" 🐾

Jason Leffler
Chloe & Daphne

"**D**aphne took some work. We were living in Anderson, Indiana, and I called a vet about finding a dog. He recommended someone for us to contact. I knew for sure we wanted a girl. We went to see the puppies, and most of them were playing together except one girl; she was just doing her own thing. Needless to say, she was our girl.

"We travel so much that at first we would leave her behind; it gave her a chance to hang out with other dogs and have some fun. But Daphne needed a buddy, a sister, someone to play with whenever she wanted. So we called the vet again and went to see more puppies. Chloe stood out. She was terrorizing the other puppies, and she was feisty.

"They get along so well now, but at first Daphne would just tolerate Chloe. She'd look up at us like, 'Who is this dog you brought home? She's bothering me!' But when we weren't looking, Daphne started to warm up to Chloe.

"They're like our children. They have the run of the household, whether it's in the bedroom with us or outside in their yard. They are so amazing. No matter what's going on, they love you. They have brought Alison and me closer together, because they are like our kids. They are so consistent in their love.

"For the most part, we don't take them to the track – so after races, we can't wait to get home and see them and be with them. We had them in Daytona and it was great! No pressure to hurry home, because our family was all together in one place; it was complete.

"We got Daphne early on in our relationship, so she's been through everything with us. She's been through a couple moves with us, and she's traveled all over the country. She loves going to the race shop; she's so content, it's like she's home. She likes to lay next to the race cars with the noise and all the activity. Daphne is a big eater, too; she once ate an entire carrot cake, including licking the plate clean as a whistle and the plate never so much as moved.

"Please take responsibility for your pet. Take them to the vet, take care of them and give them the love they so deserve. Don't let them run wild; play with them. They'll make your life so complete." 🐾

> **"They are so amazing. No matter what's going on, they love you."**

Jason Leffler pictured with wife Alison
and dogs Daphne and Chloe

Robbie Loomis
Shelter Dog, Speckles

"**I**t just blows me away how beautiful shelter animals can be. Their spirits are so full and happy. I had animals growing up and hope to again someday soon. You can see the appreciation this dog has just hanging out with me. This is appreciation and love. This is just a prime example of the kind of dog that, on any given day, you can walk into a shelter and find. To adopt an animal from a shelter is a kindhearted and fulfilling thing to do. You know they are grateful; they show it. It is a very sad state of affairs learning about all the unwanted animals that do not survive. If just a small percentage of people out looking for a pet would adopt or rescue, then that would save one of these animals from a life destined for doom.

"Animals have always been a part of who we are as people. It wouldn't be the same world without them. I know how much they have meant to me over my lifetime and the joy and laughs they can bring to your day, especially if it isn't the kind of day you necessarily wanted it to be. They are therapy for many people and can bring normalcy back into a hectic life. Please help prevent unwanted dogs and cats, and help make sure your animals and your friends' animals are spayed and neutered; then we can focus on the rest. If you aren't interested in adopting but want to help, make a donation to a local humane shelter; it will make a difference and help the crisis we're in." 🐾

Robbie Loomis pictured with Speckles, a shelter dog from the Humane Society of Concord & Cabarrus County in Concord, North Carolina (www.dogsaver.org/cabarrushumane)

Sterling Marlin
Max

"It was 1995, and on one of my many weekly flights in and out I noticed a pregnant dog at the airport. I kept seeing her around, week after week, and it became obvious that she was homeless. Finally, I noticed one day that she wasn't pregnant anymore; she had had the

puppies. I took a little time that day to see if I could locate the puppies; if she was having a hard time feeding herself, she was having a hard time feeding those puppies. After looking around, I found Max and scooped him up. I'm guessing he was only about six weeks old. That was about ten years ago, and I've had him ever since. I guess you could say I rescued him. He's a big, sweet old boy. He just hangs out here and roams the property. I think he's probably half Chow and half Golden Retriever or Lab. He's kind of shy, really.

"Max always meets me right here in the driveway. He'll see me driving down the road and he's ready for me when I pull in, tail wagging and all. Yeah, I think he probably has a real good life up here with us, and he probably knows it's better than that old airport for sure. He'll go over to the shop and hang out a little, but for the most part he's pretty independent. We have a shop cat named Deuce, and he and Max are the same color. Max doesn't even bother that cat. I don't know if one has to do with the other, but Max cannot be bothered by Deuce. It's a good life for them, and that makes me feel good."

"*He'll see me driving down the road and he's ready for me when I pull in, tail wagging and all.***"**

Mark Martin
Shelter Dog, Molly

"'**M**an's best friend' generally sums it up, especially when you're a kid. I had dogs as a kid, and there's just nothing quite like that.

"So many animals are mistreated and abused, and that is the sad and tragic thing about it. So many animals that aren't taken care of; what devastation. What a disappointment that our society could let this happen.

"These projects that raise awareness are the best vehicles I can think of. The time and caring that it takes can change quite a few minds about having a loving pet as a part of the family. Letting our fans know how much we care about this cause and that we are committed to the well-being of these furry creatures out there, well, it's just important – and personally, it's important to me.

"I know that most of the drivers have pets, and most of them travel with them. It makes the family even more of a family. I know my son would really like a dog right now, and I know he'd take really good care of it, too. They're just great companions. Love them, take care of them and most of all, be kind to them."

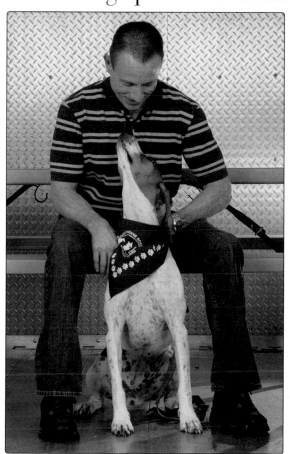

Mark Martin pictured with Molly, a shelter dog from the Cascades Humane Society in Jackson, Michigan (www.cascadeshumanesociety.com)

Jeremy Mayfield
Isabella ("Izzy"), Mattie, Max & Zoe

"**W**e wanted a dog to travel with us, but we didn't know what we wanted. We were in Loudon, New Hampshire, and walked into a pet store which has become a regular stop for us ever since. We both locked onto this Pug and kept trying to look around, but we kept going back to her. She kept staring at us, and after a little more looking around we were convinced she had to come home with us. To this day, she still gets what she wants. That's our girl, Mattie.

"Shana's mom said that Mattie needed a playmate and had a contact for a rescue that she thought would be good for us, so we got Flash. He was an older Pug and a great dog, a good companion for Mattie. He passed away last year, so we made the return trip to the same pet store in Loudon. We weren't sure what to do, but we were considering getting another dog. Well, we should know better; for sure we are going to fall in love with something walking into that store, it's a given. We had decided on this little Pug who was thin and sickly looking, with kennel cough. I was very attached immediately. Shana wasn't so sure, but I just couldn't leave without him. That's Max!

"Then – yes, that's right, we were in Loudon again! – and Shana went to look at our pet store. She fell in love, and I mean big time. Shana had a bulldog back home in Florida and fell in love with this English Bulldog, our Isabella, 'Izzy'. There's a good story there. Shana called me saying, 'You have got to see her!' so we actually didn't get her right away. We discussed it and decided that we can't have them all, and of course we would save the world if we could. Someone had put a deposit on her anyway, so we felt like we would wait and see what happened. I insisted that Shana call and check on her, and sure enough, she was still there.

"Shana played a great trick on me. She told me she didn't get her, and when we left Loudon that day and headed toward the plane, there was Izzy sitting outside the plane just waiting for me. I got teary-eyed, and we've been the best of buds ever since. We have a very special bond. She goes with me everywhere. She rides with me on the Rhino all over. She sits in the front seat of the car with me and Shana sits in the back seat! Izzy waits for me; she won't do much without me. She'll sit where she can watch for me at our front door and waits for me to come home. What a love.

"For the most part, they go with us

everywhere – but just in case, we have a 'Fur Nanny', Madeline, who takes extra-special care of them for us when necessary.

"We love the sport we're in, but it will suck the life out of you and drain you emotionally and physically. It makes you appreciate the other things in life that you love. You know, this has been good preparation for us; let's call it a 'test drive' for parenthood. We take care and nurture them just like we will our children one day. We pay attention to them so when they need something, we know it and can provide it for them. I think we get way more from them than we give to them, and that's a good deal.

"We look at these animals with great love deep down in our hearts. How can anyone abuse that? They live, they love and they have a heart and emotions. God blesses us with this special gift to respect and honor, just as he blesses us with children and family. We have to give it all the exact same respect. God meant for us to have these animals because they make our life that much more meaningful." 🐾

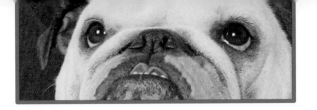

Jeremy Mayfield pictured with wife Shana and dogs
Isabella ("Izzy"), Mattie, Max and Zoe

Larry McReynolds
Fontana

" **W** e had a wonderful old Sheepdog named Samantha for about 13 years. She was our first dog together. We discussed getting another dog, but with my career, traveling the way I do, I wasn't as keen about it as Linda was. We could never really take Samantha to the track because she was so big, but we could take a small dog if we wanted to.

"It was the 2001 season; I was in Watkins Glen and my cell phone kept ringing. I glanced down to see that it was home calling, so I immediately answered. It was Linda. She had been out and had seen a dog and decided, with the help of the pet store sales pitch, that this was a great little animal – didn't shed, hypoallergenic, good disposition, smart, etc. She fell in love with him. She wanted my opinion, and I said, 'Go for it.' I came home from that trip, and there he was with a warm 'Welcome home!' at the front door.

"Fontana is a great family dog. He's mostly Linda's dog. He's a funny little guy. Linda works out in our community, and she'll walk to the gym. He knows if she's on foot that she'll be back soon, so he waits the entire time for her right by the front door until she returns. If she takes off in the car, he knows that could mean an indefinite period of time and does his own thing until she returns. I guess they were right; he's a very smart little dog. He's a creature of habit and has a great sense of who he is – he is very predictable.

Now as for the kids, our daughter, Kendall, can twist him every way, drag him around – gently, of course! – and play with him like a doll. He tolerates her every playful whim, and he's still crazy about her.

"I'm an early riser; I'm up at about 4:00, 4:30 a.m. I'll go into the kitchen for coffee, and that's his moment to get as close to Linda as he can. Now sometimes it becomes an entire family thing – and before you know it, it's the dog, Kendall and Brandon, and we're all piled in there together. I'm glad he's there, especially when I'm gone. I feel that he creates a sense of security and companionship for Linda and the kids.

"Like animals, we are all here by chance. None of us asked to be brought into this world. So there is an innocence that goes along with that. That especially goes for these stray animals out there. That doesn't mean you have to take in a stray; that just means that if a stray wandered down my driveway and looked like he hadn't been fed in days – and especially if he looked mistreated – I'd certainly make an effort to give

him food, water and comfort. I would take him where a child, family or single person could appreciate him and give him a good quality of life.

"You can go out and spend hundreds of dollars on a great pet, but you'd be amazed if you go to the shelters and see the sweet dogs and cats that so desperately need a home. We need to prevent the mistakes; it's up to us. It is much quicker and easier to take care of all of that in advance by spaying and neutering. It saves a lot of headaches and heartaches in the end. It is not any different than taking care of yourself."

"*I'm glad he's there, especially when I'm gone. I feel that he creates a sense of security and companionship for Linda and the kids.***"**

Larry McReynolds pictured with wife Linda, children Brooke, Kendall and Brandon, and dog Fontana

Casey Mears
Gus & Rags

"**I**t was a pretty cool experience getting Gus. I went to a shelter and asked my mom to come along. While I was looking around in one area of the shelter, my mom would bring over these cute little kittens. They jumped all over my lap, but none of them would just stay and hang with me. Gus happened to be in the cage right next to me, and he kept sticking his paw out trying to get my attention. He looked horrible; he had grease all over him and he had a broken tail, fleas and ringworm. He was a mess. I kept telling my mom that I wanted him, and as soon as they handed him to me, he curled up and went to sleep. I knew he was the cat I wanted, and he's been pretty cool ever since.

"When I moved to North Carolina, Jimmie Johnson had rag doll cats at the time and I really wanted one. I wanted somebody for Gus to hang out with, so I got Rags. When I first got Rags, Gus hated him – I mean, hated him. Gus had been an only child for almost six years. He was so jealous. It took him a few months, but they're the best of friends now.

"The cool thing about a cat is that they're always there when you need them. Sometimes when I come home, I'm so tired I just don't want to do anything – and they don't require anything of you. I just love the fact that they are there. They'll just curl up next to you in bed and go to sleep. When you're really up for the interaction, then they are real people cats. It's so nice to just have them here, and they really act so happy to see you, too. The undivided support from these guys is such a big part of it. I am so attached to them now. They are such a great distraction from the rest of the world.

"My mom is an animal freak and we've had everything – I mean, everything. Every kind of bird, chicken, pigs, goats, a ferret, lizards, iguanas, snakes, tarantulas, turtles, rats. We also had a dog that I loved very much named Cinder; she was a chocolate Lab and loved to eat – shall we say, she was a big dog. She'd get so happy to see you that she would shake all over and smile at the same time.

"I knew I could be a good pet parent and maintain a relationship with them, yet they could maintain their independence and me mine. It works, and I think we're all happy. You know, I think the animals that get adopted really appreciate it. Maybe check out a shelter; I think the relationship is worth the work and the investment of time, and the decision to do that is the reward." 🐾

> **"** *It's so nice to just have them here, and they really act so happy to see you, too. The undivided support from these guys is such a big part of it. I am so attached to them now.* **"**

Casey Mears pictured with Gus and Rags

Don Miller
Ellie & Freckles

"**P**at found Freckles – or should I say, Freckles found Pat! She was out on one of her walks for charity, and Freckles started following her. She appeared to be homeless but we weren't sure, so we made an attempt to find her mom and dad. Evidently she either got dropped off on the side of the road or got away. Pat brought her home, we took her in and it's been thirteen years now. We estimated she was about one when she became a member of the family. She's a Dalmatian and Lab mix from what we've been told; that one back leg is all Lab – all black!

"Ellie is our granddog. She came from our daughter, Pam, when our first grandson was about a year old. Pam was pregnant with her second child and called us with an S.O.S.: 'Mom and Dad, please help!' So we took Ellie and fell in love with her. Both Freckles and Ellie have frequent flyer miles; they really belong to the entire family.

"These guys are great companions for us and great protection with both of us traveling at different times. Us coming home is always a happy time for Freckles; she is always happy no matter what. Pam had Ellie trained but, well, you know Grandmas... they can do what they want when they want! They are both well behaved, except when Samson, the gigantic German Shepherd next door, comes out; it's a definite stare-off. They will run the line of their electric fences and make each other crazy.

"We've always had animals. When I first met Pat, she had Boots. Slowest dog in the world; you could hear her coming down the hall, drag, drag, drag, slowly, slowly. Boots was a 'Heinz 57'; she was a riot. We've always adopted and rescued. Pam found a dog in the woods when we lived in Arkansas – Patches – and when she went off to school, that was another one we inherited. We love animals.

"We let our dogs do what the family does. They ride in the cars. They come in the house. What's the use in having them if you're not going to enjoy their spirit?" 🐾

Ryan Newman
Digger, Harley, Mopar & Socks

"**W**hen I first met Krissie, I learned she was part of a package deal. She had a German Shepherd mix that she adopted while in college named Digger. She named her after Digger Phelps from ESPN. When our relationship became more serious we discussed getting Digger a companion. Well, one morning Digger took off chasing some squirrels. Finding her made both of us late for work. When she returned to the house, she was scolded and left to 'reflect' while we were out.

"On our way out, we noticed a box full of puppies on the side of the road. We both pulled over and saw that one of the puppies had tipped the whole box over. I knew at that moment we had found Digger a friend; her name became Harley. We brought her home that evening and Digger was so mad, she hasn't run off much since!

"About a year or so later, I was fishing up at our property in Statesville, North Carolina, and Krissie was in the cabin working on our future home plans. Harley and Digger heard something and took off running after it. At the same time, a guy pulled into our driveway. The dogs came running back to the house, only there was a puppy with them. The guy eventually left, and Krissie looked at me and said, 'That man forgot his dog.' He was flea infested and his hair was matted, so she quickly realized he might be a stray and convinced me to take him home. We guessed he was about four months old.

"We posted signs to see if anyone was missing this puppy. We never received one phone call; he had been abandoned. We knew then that we had a new addition to our family. Krissie decided on naming him Mopar; she says she gave him a 'manly' name so I would let her keep him. What the heck, there is always enough love at our house for a dog!

"Our latest addition came from a litter of abandoned puppies. Not far from where we live, some friends noticed a stray dog had given birth in their yard. The mother had been coming back to feed them, so we set food out for her and waited until the puppies could be weaned off of her. We took the litter to the Humane Society of Catawba County for shots and a routine check. They ended up coming home with us so we could foster them, and when they were old enough we had all four of them spayed and neutered. We contacted our family and friends and found good homes for all of the puppies… except one. I got attached to the runt of the litter and named her Socks. She became the fourth and newest member of our family.

“ *Digger was bitten by a snake near our lake home. When she was healing she developed an infection, and even with extensive treatments at NCSU vet school, she had to lose her leg. It was one of the hardest things for us to deal with. I am amazed at how well she is doing on three legs and how much happier she seems. It is almost like she was born with three legs.* ”

— *Krissie Newman*

"Usually Harley and Socks start the morning rampage by jumping on our bed to wake us up. All of them run downstairs to the door and almost knock us over trying to get outside to chase the squirrels. About ten minutes later, they are ready to come back inside and get their morning treat. They go just about everywhere when we are home; they go to the race shop, ride in the car up to our property, out to get ice cream at Bruster's, and of course, to PetsMart for treats. Our property seems to be their favorite place; they can run around, swim and chase wildlife and each other."

"Socks' latest thing is fishing. When someone catches a fish, she goes in the water and tries to get it off the hook for them. I guess you can say she prefers to catch and release! All of our dogs enjoy fishing. When it was just Digger, Harley and Mo, they would come out on our Ranger boat. One day, Digger wanted a sip of water and tried to lean over the side of the boat. I didn't notice she was doing this and when I put the motor in reverse, Digger went splashing into the water. She quickly swam to shore and ran out on someone's dock. When I got over to her, she jumped back on the boat and was ready to finish fishing. Like I said, they do everything with us – and in her case, without missing a beat.

"Krissie and I think people need to be very well educated before they go out and get a pet. Know what you are getting into. It is like having a child. When you get one, you have to keep it. It is not an option to say, 'Oh, we can't handle it going to the bathroom in the house, or chewing on the furniture.' That is what animals do. You have to be patient and teach them, like someone

66 *Our property seems to be their favorite place; they can run around, swim and chase wildlife and each other.* 99

— *Krissie Newman*

had to teach you. The most important thing is to make sure you are ready for a pet. If it's a specific kind of animal you are looking for, check your local humane society or rescue groups. Animals do not have their own birth control, so it is important to have them spayed or neutered. Over time that will help reduce the pet overpopulation problem and hopefully end euthanization. So many of these wonderful animals are euthanized, it is hard for us to grasp. We can only do what we can, but we are trying to make a difference in our community and on a national level to help lower the population of stray animals." 🐾

66Love is patient, especially when it comes to people and their pets. No matter how many mistakes you make, or how many times they run off and we have to be late because we are searching for them, we still love them – and they still love us. It is an unconditional love.99

—*Krissie Newman*

Ryan Newman pictured with wife Krissie and dogs Digger, Mopar, Socks and Harley. Also pictured is dog Panda, one of a rescued litter who has since been adopted by Krissie's mother.

Benny Parsons
Winston

"**W**hen I was a young boy, back in school, I had an unbelievable dog – a Cocker Spaniel named Pudge. From where the school bus dropped me off every day, about a half mile from where I lived, I'd walk home. The minute my house came into view, I could see Pudge sitting there in the front yard, looking toward the very spot where I'd appear. As soon as he'd see me, he'd start running toward me as hard as he could. That vision, I'll never forget. I was crazy about that dog, and he was crazy about me.

"Winston was a survivor; she literally showed up on our doorstep. There were a few little neighborhood girls who lived around the corner. They were on a walk through the woods one day and saw a plastic bag move. It scared them, and they ran off to get their dad. He went back with the girls, and he opened the bag. They figured out quickly that someone had dumped puppies. Winston was the only one that didn't get out of the bag. She was between six and seven weeks old. They put up signs all over the neighborhood trying to find a home for her. They already had three dogs of their own. The doorbell rang Monday morning, and we could have both bet a million dollars it was going to be the little girls with the puppy. Yep, it was. We'll never forget little Amanda saying, 'Oh, please, Benny, won't you take her? You know what they'll do to her if we have to take her to the pound!' So, we decided to take her. In that moment we made the commitment to make sure she was well taken care of when we were traveling. Thirty minutes later we were at Wal-Mart buying everything we could get our hands on to make her new life the best it could be.

"Fast forward to Daytona a year later. We had to be there early for work and had to leave Winston at the vet's. We were gone for almost four weeks, so the following year we went back to Daytona and decided to look for a condo. Need I say more? We wanted Winston to be with us; no more leaving her with the vet. It was a very humbling moment when I had to admit to the realtor that I was buying a condo for my dog. She has one beautiful dog house in Daytona, that's for sure. She's been ruling the house ever since.

"Winston loves to be outside. We want her to safely enjoy being outside, so we have a very long lead, maybe 25 feet or more. From time to time she'll go hang out, guard the house, and watch the passersby. Well, one Christmas I looked out, and no Winston. Panic set in; we

dashed around calling for her, looking for her. We took the car out scoping the neighborhood, and just as we're coming around the corner we see our neighbor looking toward our house with her hands covering her face. Our hearts sank. What had happened to Winston? As we pulled up, we saw Winston wrapped from head to toe in Christmas lights and every decoration you

can think of, including candy canes. She had somehow pulled her lead out, probably chasing a squirrel, and tore through the neighbor's yard, completely destroying his decorations. She had all of them in tow, caught up in her 25-foot lead. It was a sight to behold and one we'll never forget. She has been the best dog, though. That's about as bad as it got.

"The dog takes our minds off everything else that's going on in our lives. She's a complete change of attitude and personality. To us she's like our child, because she requires almost constant attention. She can't open a door by herself. She can't open a can of dog food and mix a meal by herself. So there are things that require attention and details.

"We found out, soon after we bought our 'dog house' in Daytona, that we weren't the only animal lunatics in racing. We knew a team owner who flew his dogs around and didn't mind kicking somebody off to get his animals a seat on the plane. We knew we weren't alone. I told that same guy that we were headed to get Winston chicken before we left for the next race. The guy said, 'What, Alpo?' I said, 'No, Harris Teeter.'

"We've got to slow down. The overpopulation has gotten completely out of hand. Every person who has an animal has to dedicate a part of their lives to them. They need to take the responsibility of spaying and neutering them.

"Patience is a gift. Having a dog, or any kind of pet, brings you back to reality. It makes you slow down a little bit and take things the way they really are. It's such a pure love; they take you just the way you are. The capacity they have for love should be honored always. Look at this dog and the love she has brought us. She came out of the woods in a plastic bag. Look to adopt or rescue first, before anything. It has been one of the biggest rewards of our life." 🐾

> **"**It was a very humbling moment when I had to admit to the realtor that I was buying a condo for my dog.**"**

Benny Parsons pictured with wife Terri and dog Winston

Kyle and Pattie Petty pictured with dogs Spurs and Mattie, donkey Ellie Mae, horses Chip and Hawk, and campers
at Victory Junction Gang Camp in Randleman, North Carolina (www.victoryjunction.org)

Kyle Petty
Chip, Ellie Mae, Hawk, Mattie & Spurs

"**W**e're in the horse business, and we've never sold a horse. We're in the cow business, and we've never sold a cow. We're in the goat business, and we've never sold a goat. We can't. If you want one, we'll give one to you, though. We have 47 animals altogether.

Spurs was a gift from God. Our daughter, Montgomery Lee, was in a horse show, and in all rights she should have won. Her heart was broken. I was a spoiled-rotten kind of mother, and in that moment I said, 'Montgomery Lee, you can have any puppy you want.' She picked out a Miniature Australian Shepherd. We didn't know anything about the breed, and the woman we were buying her from started to tell us that these dogs were similar to a Border Collie – which just happened to be a dog that I had wanted because of all the horses and goats. She continued to tell us that they would work your horses and animals, too, just not quite as hard.

"As Spurs grew up, everybody fell in love with him. I kept the woman's card, and along the way I have bought 18 dogs from her as gifts. We gave Tony Stewart one. We got off the plane and heard Tony had won the IROC race, so we ran to Victory Lane and gave him Checkers. My daughter really wanted for Tony to have one, because anybody who knows Tony loves Tony.

"We used to be able to spend more time with Spurs and Mattie, but now we're at camp so much. They live in the barn and take care of everything. If we get home before dark, we'll go down to the lodge on our property and water the flowers, and they just love the creek. We have a 48-acre lake, and Spurs and Mattie love to swim, too.

"We also have an old German Shepherd named Digger and a big old Lab named Cletus. They run the farm; they take care of everything, too. They wouldn't hurt a flea; they are so totally dependent upon us. They can't communicate to you what they feel; you have to read it in their eyes. I find that extremely intriguing.

"I find animals so brilliant; they are so intuitive with the kids here at Victory Junction Gang Camp. An animal can sense a need better than we can. There was a child here at camp last summer with an enormous brain tumor, and Chip, one of our horses, just loved him. It was the kind of memory for that child of comfort and love in a time of physical distress – what a beautiful escape, thanks to Chip.

> 66 *What these animals do for us, and what we see them do for these children here at Victory Junction, is a miracle in itself.* 99

VICTORY JUNCTION GANG

Founded for kids in honor of Adam Petty

"Our animals all have trainers. Denise is the best; they wouldn't be here without her. She works with them day in and day out so that they act the way they do. They stay in training; they have to. We love being around them because they are brilliant creatures. We have the utmost respect for God's creatures. What these animals do for us, and what we see them do for these children here at Victory Junction, is a miracle in itself.

"I can just sit and watch a cluster of horses out in the pasture. There's an old saying that there is something about the outside of a horse that makes the inside of a person feel good. There is just something so calming, so soothing about that.

"We know our limits. We cannot take care of 47 animals, which is why we have Denise; otherwise, they would not get the proper care. You don't just go to a shelter, pick out a dog or cat and expect it to adapt to your schedule. It requires training, work, patience and love.

"We would never encourage anyone to get an animal if they are not willing to change their world for it. Be ready to face the challenges — because if you're not geared up for it, you are doing that animal a grave injustice. Donate money instead; it does make a difference, a big difference."

As told by Kyle and Pattie Petty 🐾

Richard Petty
Little Queen Victoria ("Queenie") & Sir Walter Raleigh ("Raleigh")

"Kyle's daughter, our granddaughter Montgomery Lee, is into horses, and I went to a horse show with her in Raleigh. There were Corgi puppies there. About that time, Richard and I swore we would never have another dog because we had just lost our little Dachshund; we just get so attached. It kills you when they go. I saw those little puppies and I said to myself, I just can't leave here without one. So we ended up taking Raleigh home with us. I got him there, so I named him after Raleigh. I only bred him once. I chose Victoria out of his litter, so she is his daughter. We call her 'Queenie' – she's Queen Victoria.

"They are good, smart dogs, and they run this place; they keep everything and everyone in line, including the buffalo. They give those creatures a good telling to if need be! Their nature is that of hunting dogs. They were used in the English countryside to herd sheep and cows by nipping at their heels, so it helps that they are so close to the ground and that they're born with no tails."

As told by Lynda Petty

"When I come home off the road, these dogs see me coming and are ready and waiting the minute I open the car door. They jump in every

Richard Petty pictured with wife Lynda and dogs Queenie and Raleigh

time, every time! The second that door opens, there they are with their paws up on the floorboard. Now that's a warm welcome, it's a given.

"You know, it's fine to want a pet, and it's fine to have one. It's unheard of to continue to let animals breed. You have to take care of them like anything else you possess. They need to be controlled like people. We have laws and we have boundaries, so it is up to us to make good decisions for our animal world. For Lynda and me, it's a privilege."

As told by Richard Petty 🐾

Craig Reynolds
Binah, Cooper, Memnoch & Vivian

"**I** was racing bikes, and we were at the track watching Animal Planet. The show was 'Emergency Vet' – and need I say more, the dog died. The very next day we were at the mall and Tisha said, 'Let's go see the puppies!' I am a sucker for cute things. There was Vivian, rolling around and playing with her brothers and sisters. She stops, looks at us and, well, that was pretty much it. We got her out of the cage and started playing with her. She was so cute and so playful. She fell right to sleep in my lap. We named her Vivian. She had us at hello!

"We had rescued a male Lab right before we moved to North Carolina. His name was Raleigh. He was so protective; he was amazing, the star pupil at his obedience class. Raleigh would patrol the neighborhood. He knew everybody and watched over us like a hawk. He started having seizures because a tumor started to grow on his forehead. It was cancer. It was a great year for us, because he showed us so much by just being him.

"Vivian was very affected by the loss of Raleigh, so we started looking online on Petfinder. com. We found this yellow Lab, and Tisha went to see him. When she got home, she said, 'You've got to go see this guy, he is really good looking.' His parents had gone through a divorce, and they needed to give him up. I went back with Tisha and took one look at him and said, 'That's a Dane.' Sure enough, he was part Lab and part Great Dane. Cooper, the great 'Dane-e-ator'! This guy will crack you up. You know he knows how to speak; I'm just waiting!

"I love hanging with these guys. They look at me like, 'It's Dad! He's home!' You can't beat that. Tisha had the two cats before 'us' and I am allergic, but there was no way I could say they had to go. They just make you a more compassionate person. They live in the moment – again, how great is that?

"You don't always have to go with a puppy; that's where I think a lot of people get into trouble. If you want a particular dog, there are rescues for all types of breeds. Adoption is a great way to go. Cooper, our rescue, is amazing. It made us feel better knowing our money was going to a rescue. We will continue to rescue and our family will continue to grow." 🐾

Craig Reynolds pictured with dogs Vivian and Cooper

Doug Richert

Allie, Benji, Daisy, Harry, Ivey, May, Morris, Nash, OJ, Oscar #2, Pedo, Pee Wee, Petunia, Porky, Sasha & Stevie

"We found our Husky, Harry, on the side of the road. He was skin and bones, dehydrated and had the mange with ticks all over his body. We dropped him off at the vet for some TLC, and three days later he had gained twelve pounds and was ready to begin a new life. He's been with us ever since.

"Our first dog together was Oscar #1 in 1985. Then there was Frisky, Bozo, Suzi, Randy, Checkers and more. We love animals more than anything. Oscar #2 is 17, OJ is 15, and Benji is 12. Then came the Pugs – their mom died giving birth, so we hand-fed them for weeks 'round the clock. Pee Wee came into the picture two years ago, and Sasha was next. A friend found her in the middle of the road and dropped her off here with us. Then there was Stevie; a friend at the vet's office knew we had lost a Border Collie and called me about Stevie – what's one more?

"Then there are the cats. Nash came from Nashville. He was almost dead when we found him, and we nursed him back to health; he was only two weeks old when we found him. Then there's Petunia, Allie and Ivey… whew!

"You know, we can wreck, we can blow up at the track and they will still kiss you and love you and look for attention. They know nothing about racing and they don't care; they know about love, devotion and food!

"It's very important that people are aware of what it takes to take care of a pet – the responsibility and the financial commitment. Donate money to a local shelter; it will help with spay and neuter expenses. We can't stress the importance of that enough. We think that when you respect an animal, you respect a human being a lot more, too. The way people treat their pets is usually the way they treat others. We think we're pretty good people. If we can help a dog, we hope that makes us pretty good people.

"We wish – and we've discussed this many times – that children in school would be educated about how to take care of and treat their animals. They are a life, and that life needs to be taken care of.

"Our entire family makes this happen for us. We couldn't do it without them. Robin's mom and her sister, Angie, help take care of all of them. Robin's mom has been helping for more than 20 years now. It's a family affair and that's the way it should be, because we all love them so much and appreciate what they bring to our lives."

You know, we can wreck, we can blow up at the track and they will still kiss you and love you and look for attention. They know nothing about racing and they don't care; they know about love, devotion and food!

Doug Richert pictured with wife Robin and dogs Benji, Pedo, May, Sasha, Daisy and PeeWee.

Ricky Rudd
Cali & Koda

"**W**e were interested in Bengal cats. We wanted something a little different and unique, and Ricky has always liked big, spotted cats. I just happened to notice in the paper an ad for a 'dog in a cat suit'. They act like dogs, they really do. Bengal cats fetch and catch and are really playful. So we investigated a little bit more and ended up getting Koda, a spotted brown Bengal. We found Koda in the Lake Norman area of North Carolina.

"We'd had Koda for about a year and a half, and while we were in Daytona for the Daytona 500, I sat down at my computer one day and Googled 'Bengal cats' for the heck of it. See, Ricky always wanted to take Koda to the track and I would say no. I was real insistent that he stay with my son and me. For the most part, we go to the track with the exception of the rare schedule conflict. So I Googled on my little laptop, 'Bengal Cats Florida', and one popped up. It happened to be right down the street. It was meant to be. She was a little brown marbled Bengal, and that's what we wanted. I went to see her and as I watched her, I knew her disposition was so sweet. I said, 'She's the perfect cat for us and for Koda.' They are perfect for one another. They play, tumble and roll; they really do have fun together. Koda will chase you like a dog, and he'll let you chase him.

"We have a farm, and one day Ricky called me from the barn and said, 'Come down here, you've got to see this.' I picked up our son, Landon, at school and immediately headed to the barn – only to find five little kitties about four weeks old. They were very sick, with runny noses and goopy eyes, so I called the vet right away. We got the proper medication and nursed them back to health. It was a crazy week – it was Charlotte race week, so in addition to being a busy time of the year, we had to bottle-feed these little kittens and give them as much love and care as possible. We got them all litter box trained and eating and drinking, and in 10 days we found good homes for all of them. We were so proud of our accomplishment.

"To us, we consider animals to be just like people. That's why we offered help to the small kitties, so they could have a good life. You need

to take care of a situation if it presents itself to you. Treat the animals the same way you would treat your children. If being a pet parent doesn't suit you and your lifestyle, then don't do it – but you can always help an animal find a home. It was work for us, but we did it. Take the time to care; it does make a difference."

As told by Linda Rudd 🐾

“*I just happened to notice in the paper an ad for a 'dog in a cat suit'. They act like dogs, they really do.*”

Ricky Rudd pictured with wife Linda and cats Koda and Cali

Elliott Sadler
Chelsea & Hard Rock

"**I**'ve been part of a big deer hunting family and an outdoorsman all my life. My dad used to take me when I was a kid. It's something I still do with family and friends. It's time away from the racetrack and away from all the media and city stuff. It's great therapy. I can be me, Elliott Sadler from Emporia, Virginia – not Elliott Sadler, the race car driver.

"We've hunted our whole lives, and we just decided about 15 years ago that we would raise our own dogs. I love them to death. If someone came to me tomorrow and said we couldn't raise dogs or use them to hunt, I don't think I'd ever hunt again. It's a love; they're my kids. I'm not married and I don't have any kids; these dogs are my kids. When they do a good job and perform for you, you're like a proud papa.

"They are so loving, and they recognize you the minute you come home. What they do for me is absolutely amazing. They are there for your every beck and call. It is just great to get away from the high-stress, fast-paced world of racing and come back home to Emporia, out here in the country where I was born and raised. It's just a relaxing feeling; there's so much more comfort to be had around people you grew up with. I've tried to explain that to people for years, why I still live here; but until you come here and see what the dogs do, where they live, where I live and you actually experience it, you may never understand.

"There is not a better feeling or sound to me in the world than when my dogs get together and work together. You can hear them barking and running; it's unbelievable. I just can't explain it.

"Being in the public eye all the time, we can set a good example about how you are supposed to treat people and how you're supposed to treat animals. How can you look at a dog or a cat or an animal and not love them? They are such loving, caring creatures and honest beings; they don't know the problems of the world or what we're going through. As far as I'm concerned, they're just man's best friend. Everyone I know, friends and family alike, takes good care of their animals. We love and take care of each and every one of them. That is very important and very special to us. I'll never sell one, never. I'll give you a dog, but never will I sell. I love them and love being around them." 🐾

There is not a better feeling or sound to me in the world than when my dogs get together and work together. You can hear them barking and running; it's unbelievable. I just can't explain it.

Dogs run in the family – Elliott's dad, Herman Sadler, Jr. (right), pictured years ago with one of many family dogs and family friend Warren Rawlings

Kenny Schrader
Goblin

"It was Halloween night, 1987, and we were out at T-Bone's Steakhouse in Phoenix, Arizona. This black cat was there, and Ann wanted to take her home. I said no because we were leaving to go to Riverside, California, to a race. So I said, 'I'll tell you what, if she's there tomorrow night, we'll get her.' The next night, sure enough, she was there. We found her going through the dumpster; she was just a little thing then. We named her Goblin – seemed like the perfect name, with Halloween and being a black cat and all.

"I had a friend who said that she was wild and would be hard to handle, hard to tame and most likely wouldn't be living indoors. So that night we bought a Styrofoam cooler, took the lid off and made her a litter box. We dumped her in there a few times before getting her back home, and she adapted just fine.

"Our friends drove Goblin to Riverside, and then we had to buy her an airline ticket home. At the time, Michael Waltrip was single and traveling alone, and he just happened to be on the same flight as Goblin – so he took care of Goblin all the way home. The flight attendants went nuts; good-looking, single Michael Waltrip and a beautiful cat wasn't a bad deal at the time!

"I'm actually allergic to cats, but she's been a good one. I put up with the itching, no problem. We've rescued many cats; they are all over the shop. Ann and I pay to have them fixed and find them good homes. It's also kind of a neighborhood thing, too; we'll feed them, fix them and make sure we find them good homes and good parents.

"Goblin grew up with our kids. She's been with us longer than our kids have been with us. We love animals and love having them in our lives. Ann's family always had animals growing up, and she says they are just 'natural lovers' – they just blend into your family." 🐾

Kenny Schrader with wife Ann, son Sheldon, daughter Dorothy and cat Goblin

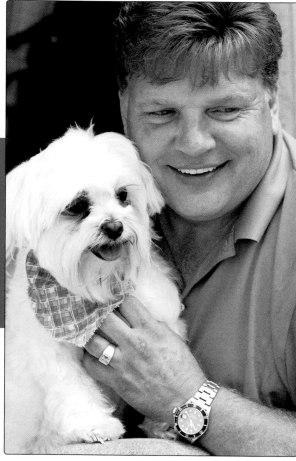

Jimmy Spencer
Dharma, Oscar, Princess, Sabrina & Zippo

"When the kids were growing up, we had a Golden Retriever named Butch. He got very old and had cancer. The vet helped me out so much when it was time to let Butch go. He said, 'Tell the kids that he never woke up.' It was the best advice; it's much less painful that way for children.

"Shortly after, we found Princess under a sign that said, '$10.00, sold'. Jimmy, our son, had to have her. She's incredible.

"I was in Miami racing in a Busch race. I always wanted a black Schnauzer. My sister happened to go to the mall in Concord, North Carolina, and there was a black Schnauzer. We got him and named him Zippo, after the car I was racing at the time. He was supposed to be my dog, but Pat fell in love with him.

"I guess it was right around Christmas when we got Sabrina. So then we had Princess, Zippo and Sabrina. Our daughter, Katrina, felt left out; she wanted a dog. I was out playing golf one day, and they decided that it was time for Katrina to go out and get a dog. I come home, and now we have Oscar! He has become my favorite. Maltese are people; they are so smart.

"One day we were at the beauty shop with all our babies. A lady came in who knew Pat had been interested in a white Schnauzer. So then we got Dharma. The best thing about Dharma is I can't go anywhere without her. I wake up and go to get the paper, and she comes with me. She watches me put on my shoes. She monitors my every move. I just love her. You've never seen anything like her in your life.

"One day I was playing with her, and I felt something in her throat. We took her to the vet and found out that she has lymphoma; it's cancer. We're doing everything we can; she's getting treatments. The prognosis is never good in these cases, but I believe she's going to be the exception. She has all these great dogs around her and her family that loves her so much. I'm thinking another year. She's in remission right now.

"We had a shelter dog, Babe, that belonged to my son Jimmy. I just don't understand how people can abandon dogs. I can't figure out how people can abuse dogs. My dad helped me train my dogs at a young age. The biggest mistake people make is not training their dogs. We've had so many wonderful dogs - Butch, Freckles. It makes a grown man cry when he loses a dog; you're losing a family member.

"I can't wait to get home and greet my babies; it's awesome. There's nothing better than walking into your house and seeing them waiting for you, tails wagging. They know if you don't want to be bothered; they are so smart. I must admit, we spoil them with love and treats.

"There is nothing like a dog to take a walk with, to go outside with, or just sit by you. They are the best release for stress in the world, in my opinion. For all the NASCAR fans out there, if you're looking for a dog or cat, go to the shelters. Check them out regularly; there will be more every day. Don't be afraid to help save a life. Our ten dollars for Princess went a very long way. The amount of animals that are being put down is intolerable, insane. After you get one, you'll want two, then three. You'll see."

66*There is nothing like a dog to take a walk with, to go outside with, or just sit by you. They are the best release for stress in the world, in my opinion.*99

Jimmy Spencer pictured with wife Pat, son Jimmy, daughter Katrina, and dogs Princess, Sabrina, Zippo, Dharma, and Oscar

Tony Stewart
Kayle

"We were in Daytona, and we had just finished the Rolex 24 Hour race. I had to come back home and get a physical, so we flew back to Charlotte. I had a 400-gallon fish tank, and the guy that comes to service it happens to be right near my doctor's office. He had called and told me that he had gotten a new shipment of exotic fish, so I decided to go over and give it a look. There's a room near where I was headed to look at the fish, and as I was going that direction, I saw this great big cage off to the right. I looked down and there Kayle was, smaller than the palm of my hand, so I just stopped and looked at her. I'd been interested in Chihuahuas for a while. She didn't bark; she just looked at me while she played with a toy. Not so much as a peep came out of her. I went and looked at the fish and decided to go back and take another look at her. Kayle walked toward the end of the cage, stood up and just looked at me. She was so calm for a puppy, and for a Chihuahua. So I spent another half hour just watching her. I kept thinking that there was really something different about her. Needless to say, I ended up taking her and the cage back to Florida that night.

"Kayle is a great companion and a great travel dog. She knows the airplane when she sees it; she's there before I am. She doesn't get nervous and doesn't ever get sick. She's the perfect pet. I can pick her up with one hand. When we're in a 45-foot motor home for three days, I can sit in the front of the bus and throw her toys and I don't have to worry about her not getting enough exercise. She makes it very easy to travel with her; she's very social and loves people.

"She's a Chihuahua, but she thinks she's a Lab. When we're at home in Indiana, I have 400 acres with an eight-acre lake. Most Chihuahuas won't get near the water, but she'll go right down to the lake and splash around in the water. Kayle acts like a Lab.

"It doesn't matter what kind of day I've had on the racetrack or at home. Kayle helps change my mood in a hurry. It gets me back to being grounded, helps level me emotionally. She's a huge part of my weekend. Every emotion from these animals is an honest one; they are just so happy to have your attention and affection. Kayle can tell if I'm worn out or frustrated after a race; she'll just jump up on my lap or lay down on my chest. She is so good at sensing my mood.

"Kayle doesn't care what we're doing; she just loves to be outside. If we go to the racetrack, she wants to go; if we're going four-wheeling, she wants to go. She wants to be with me all the time.

"I watch Animal Planet religiously. I am a big fan. I watch the rescues quite a bit. Sure, animals can survive without us, but when they are domesticated and used to being part of a family they depend on you for their needs – to be loved and fed and exercised. If you do that, the rewards are endless. If you want a good pet, you have to put forth the effort. You love them like a kid. We all have our faults; they are not always going to be perfect, and we're not always going to be perfect either – so we need to deal with their faults. Lord knows they learn to deal with ours.

"Some people treat animals like they are toys, but they are living, breathing organisms. They have the same needs and desires we have. There is a lot of responsibility that goes along with owning a pet of any kind, whether domestic or exotic. So many people neglect that responsibility, and as a result we have too many homeless and abandoned pets. It doesn't take much if everyone will do their part. It doesn't take but a little bit of effort. Please take the time to spay or neuter your pet and do your part to help control the population." 🐾

It doesn't matter what kind of day I've had on the racetrack or at home. Kayle helps change my mood in a hurry.

Brian Vickers
Caesar

"**I** moved away from home when I was still in high school. A friend and I moved to Greensboro, North Carolina. Both my friend and I wanted a pet, but my schedule especially didn't allow for taking a dog out and giving it the attention it needs. I'd never had a cat and never was around them much, either. Cats are more self-sufficient. I made a connection with a woman who breeds Siamese cats. I thought they were very interesting, so I called her; she just so happened to be in Greensboro, so it worked out perfectly.

"I didn't know what to expect of a cat, but he's really sweet. Ever since he was a baby, he's been like a playful dog, really. He loves to play; he plays with dogs and cats and anybody he can make friends with. Caesar made it really easy to transition from dogs to cats, so all you dog lovers, who knows? You just may find great companionship in a cat.

"He hangs out with me, and when he looks at me with that loving look that all pets seem to have for their parents, he turns the day around. He really caught me off guard, because I never was a cat person. He changed my mind. I have this guy to be responsible for; he's a living being, and it's a whole different responsibility.

"You ever hear of curiosity killing the cat? Well, if he's guilty of one thing, it may be that he loves me too much. He always wants to be right in your face. When you sleep, he wants to lay right in your face. I move him and he comes right back. When you're trying to eat or work on the computer, he wants to be right in the middle. He's very clingy. I can't even go to the bathroom without Caesar's unprecedented curiosity. If he's not in the same room as you, he'll paw and whine until you let him in.

"Making sure Caesar was fixed was a priority. I didn't want him running around making unwanted kittens. He's an indoor cat, but if he got out, there is no telling what could happen. My mom set a great example with me and a dog we had growing up; she bred her once, gave all her friends the puppies and spayed her right away. We can usually thank our parents for good examples well set, so take good care to oversee all your animals' special needs. Make sure they get to the vet regularly and love them the best you can. It shows in the love they give back." 🐾

Kenny Wallace
Ellie Mae & Mac

"**W**e had a German Shepherd, our first one, and we named him after Kim's uncle, Willie Mae, who had just died from cancer. We had just put up a very expensive fence, but we had not quite finished it. It was a hot, hot summer day, so I took Willie Mae off his lead and let him run. See, I grew up in the country and I think animals should be free, not chained up or fenced in. You learn from your mistakes, and that day I made a terrible, terrible mistake. Willie Mae was chasing a butterfly and chased it right out into the street and got hit by a car.

"About two weeks after that, Kim came home with another German Shepherd, Ellie Mae. She just kept clinging to Kim, so she thought, 'Okay, this is the one.' We love her; we even cut out part of our porch so she could come up and be part of our family.

"Kim's mom and dad live in the house behind us, and I catch them every once in a while giving Ellie Mae ice cream. I yell to them, 'No, no, no ice cream!' I make Ellie a healthy batch of what I call 'goulash', dry dog food and canned dog food all mixed together. She loves it.

"We acquired Mac when our oldest, Brooke, brought him home. Brooke's getting older and testing the waters with us. She just got a nose ring, and along with that came Mac, the Chihuahua. Brooke really wanted a little dog, and he's actually become everybody's dog; Kim thinks he's a person. When we come home, Mac goes nuts. He just flies down our hallway, he's that excited.

"I know in my heart that I'm a loving, caring person. I like to look everybody in the eye, and I want everybody to get along. I have third child syndrome; it's my brother Rusty, my brother Mike and me. It's just my nature to want to take care of things; I'm a caretaker. Another good thing is if my wife and kids are mad at me, I always have the dogs, because I'm the only guy!

"Our dogs are a part of our family. When the girls go to bed, Mac is always with Kim; he never wants to leave her. Kids, dogs, it's all the same to us. We go out of our way to take care of these dogs. I make sure in the winter Ellie has her bed made, the heat on and the country music playing; it makes the ambiance just right.

"Every citizen has to make it a point to help, even if you don't personally want or have an animal. If your lifestyle doesn't allow for a pet and you have one, do not abandon it. Do the right thing and donate it to a shelter or your vet to make sure it is placed in a good, loving home. It's as simple as that." 🐾

Kenny Wallace pictured with dogs Mac and Ellie Mae

Darrell Waltrip
Daisy, Ethan Joe, Hobie Cat, L.B., Olivia & Trusty

"**C**harlie Brown – what a character! We used to sneak him into the track. He wore a flea collar, and in those days it was a round disc with little holes in it. Everyone accused me of wiring the dog and sending him around the track to pick up important information, like a spy. Not so! Sorry folks, just a flea collar.

"My horse's name is L.B., because in 1987 we were racing Chevrolet Luminas; they've since been replaced with the Monte Carlos. I wanted to connect the horse with racing, so I named him Lumina Bay.

"We had a Bassett Hound named Prissie, whom we dearly loved. When she died, I said, 'No more. I can't take it.' After two years with no dog, we agreed as a family we would start looking for another. One day Jessica and Stevie took a walk through the neighborhood. They saw three little puppies just pop right out of the woods. They called to them but the puppies were afraid; they had obviously been abandoned. The girls came home and told me, and out they went again to bring them home. Only one could be found at that point, and we named her Daisy. Here she is today.

"One day Stevie and I were in the mall and I came upon Bassett Hounds. She couldn't even look at Bassetts, but somehow I convinced her – and home we went with Olivia and Trusty.

They've been true blue and we love them.

"After our 18-year-old cat was killed, we went to animal control and found Hobie Cat. He was calm and docile and really a great cat. When we got him home, we found out that his femur was completely broken. After his surgery and recovery, he changed completely. He went from being this nice, sweet cat to Dennis the Menace. Rest assured, whatever you're doing he'll be right in the middle of it.

"For 18 years, all Stevie and I had were animals, no kids, so you just can't put into words how much peace and joy they've brought us over the years. They were our kids. I can just look at Trusty and he cheers me up; now that's something. That's why I love animals; they're your buddies. We treat them like kids. Charlie Brown slept in bed with us. You get up with them in the middle of the night and let them out; they're a lot of responsibility, and you've got to take good care of them.

"It's a terrible day when one goes. We have an animal cemetery where we've buried all of them with plaques that mark their graves. You

treat your loved ones with total respect. They have their place in the world, and they should never be mistreated.

"Most of the drivers have really soft hearts, but they can't let you see that side of them at the track because they're so competitive and such tough guys. Even Earnhardt was that way. The Intimidator, as rough and tough as he portrayed himself to be, I'd see the soft side of him when I was with him.

"The humane society is the best place in the world to get a dog or a cat. They just want a family to be a part of. The shelter and the people who work there are my heroes. I am so proud of what they do to help save every animal they can. I'm a big believer in having a passion for something. I have a passion for racing and animals. I give them all my heart and soul."

    "I can just look at Trusty and he cheers me up; now that's something. That's why I love animals; they're your buddies."

Darrell Waltrip pictured with wife Stevie, daughter Jessica, dogs Daisy, Olivia, and Trusty, and cats Hobie Cat and Ethan Joe

Michael Waltrip
Beavis, Dixie & Phoebe

"**B**eavis is from Kentucky. He was a birthday present from my friend Jeff. He was a surprise, a big surprise, and I just love him. I've had him since 1994, when he was just a puppy. He's been a real special part of the family for a long time now. Beavis moans and talks. You can really get him going, and he'll talk up a storm. He's a little higher maintenance, because if you're going to hang out with him you've got to pet him constantly; he's really needy.

"He's my dog completely, but he's also the shop dog. We have a race shop out back, and when I'm gone, Beavis will go check on the guys a lot. There will be a lot of people who argue that he's their dog, but he's my dog!

"Beavis makes me feel better about myself and life in general. He's been around for 12 years now; he's a constant in my life. When I come home, when I leave, it's always the same, happy Beav. Beavis makes me smile. He doesn't do anything wrong anymore; he's an old man now.

"If you have a dog or a cat and you go out of your way to get one, you've got to go out of your way to take care of them. They need attention, they need love and they need to be held. You are their life.

"Animals are a big part of our world. If you see one on the side of the road, stop and help it. Always do the right thing by an animal, because what you get back is a gift you can't get at any store."

When I come home, when I leave, it's always the same, happy Beav. Beavis makes me smile.

Michael Waltrip pictured with wife Buffy, daughters Macy
and Caitlin, and dogs Beavis, Dixie and Phoebe

Scott Wimmer
Reily

"**O**ur first dog was a Saint Bernard, and then we had three German Shepherds before we got Reily. I was 18 and racing local short tracks around Wisconsin. We didn't have a dog at the time. Good friends of ours raised yellow Labs. They would always bring their Labs to the track. They ended up having a litter, and Reily was the last one in the litter.

"I asked my dad that night, if I won the race, would he buy me the Lab puppy? I wanted him; he was such a cool dog. I ended up not winning; I was second. The next night I went to the track and I won, so I said, 'Now can you buy me the dog?' My dad said, 'That wasn't the deal.' Two weeks passed and he finally bought me the dog. It almost killed me; I thought I wasn't going to get him. My dad brought him to the track for me. When we first saw him, he could have fit in the palm of my hand. When they brought him back, his legs were hanging down; he'd grown about two feet, it seemed, over those two weeks.

"He's a big guy now. He travels with us, and he kind of eats what we do. He really likes pizza.

"When I moved to North Carolina, I didn't take him because he was so comfortable with my parents; he loves it there. They have land and a pond, and he just loves being outside and being lazy. I have a lot of nieces and nephews back home, and they just love him. I felt like I had to give to him what he's always given to me – a lot of happiness.

"My parents bring him to the races, so he's never that far away, thank goodness. He's a great dog. He likes to lie on the couch, and he's taken on all our family habits, good and bad. When we're not racing, we like to just hang out and look for things to do, and he's just one of the family. He's an unbelievable dog for what he's done for us. He'll paw at you, even hug you; it just makes the bad stuff go away and puts a smile on your face.

"We always thought it would be neat to have a trained dog, but we decided to let them be what they decided to be; that is something they taught us. They wanted to be themselves and who they were. In those faces are their personalities and what they stand for. He does a lot for us.

"Spaying and neutering is so important. We have a huge overpopulation problem in Wisconsin with dogs and cats. It's out of control. You don't want animals suffering and running free because of human neglect. I think adopting a pet is one of the most awesome things you can do. My wife and I go down to the shelter and take canned food and play with them; they need that interaction and love, and it makes us and them feel good. I highly recommend adopting."

Matt Yocum
Gipper

"**I**'ve had dogs all my life. In fact, the second word I ever spoke was 'dog-gee'. I gave my mom a real scare when I was 22 months old. I could see my dog outside, so I pushed my toy box up against the wall by the window and pushed the window screen out. When she came in the room I was missing, and then she noticed the screen and looked out the window. She almost had a heart attack when she saw me running in the backyard with my dog.

"We picked up Clancy (a blonde Cocker) in 1985; he was a member of our family for 14 years. When I got out of college, he moved with me through my early jobs in TV. He had an endless supply of energy and loved pizza. When he passed away, it was tough because he was my little buddy, a real trooper. You go through a tough mourning process, which I think you have to go through because they are a member of the family.

"After a couple years, I started talking to my mom about wanting another dog. She knew of a breeder in Oklahoma who had a litter of Cockers. Jan Taylor called me on my cell while I was driving back to my hotel from Michigan International Speedway. I pulled over to the side of the road; we talked for about 45 minutes about her puppy. She asked me all kinds of questions trying to find out my background and see if I was good enough for her puppy. I told her to call Dr. Jeff Cooper, Clancy's vet from the day he was born until he died. She said his parents were champion show dogs with great personalities, but he was too small to show. She added that he was the sweetest puppy in the bunch, and one more thing: 'He loves pizza.' What she didn't know was he would end up loving McDonald's french fries, too. The pictures she sent were titled 'Red Faced Boy'. He was blonde with a lot of red markings throughout his face. She shipped him to me on Delta in September 2002.

"We named him Gipper after my favorite president, Ronald Reagan. The Gipper is completely opposite of Clancy in a number of ways. Clancy was full of energy at 6:30 a.m., while Gipper is nocturnal. He'll wake up and stagger from my bed to his bed in my office. He'll sleep until around 9:00 a.m., then eat breakfast and go back to sleep until noon. We are like Butch Cassidy and the Sundance Kid. Wherever I go, he has to go, too. He would rather sleep in the truck for two hours while I am in a restaurant than sit at home. He loves to ride with his two front paws on the center console and his hind legs on the back seat so he can see out the windshield. I've taken him with me everywhere. He flies on the charter service that all the teams use; he just sits in the big chair with us or on my lap. At the race tracks he loves to sit and look out the window of the motorcoach. On walks, he is so social; he has to stop and visit with every single person sitting outside motorcoaches. He has a number of buddies whom you have read about in this book. The hanging-out factor with Gipper is awesome; he is my buddy, my 'wing-man'.

"If there are a couple things that I could change concerning pets, I wish people would spay and neuter their pets. The overpopulation problem continues to spiral out of control. Second, stronger laws need to be enacted concerning the abuse of animals. It breaks your heart when you see stories on the news about abused pets and the person gets off with a slap on the wrist. Thankfully, Animal Planet does a great job getting the awareness out there." 🐾

Acknowledgements

The making of *Pit Road Pets* was a team effort of numerous animal lovers who believed in our mission. We greatly appreciate everyone who helped us along the way.

To the drivers, crew chiefs and NASCAR personalities who took time out of their incredibly busy schedules for our photo shoots and interviews, we would like to give our most sincere appreciation. This book would be nothing but empty pages without you. Thank you for filling the pages of *Pit Road Pets* with beautiful photos and stories about you and your furry families.

We would like to thank all of the people who helped us schedule and organize the photo shoots for *Pit Road Pets*, including Gary Ahlers, Dale Cagle, Angie Copen, Van Colley, Joe Crowley, Mike Davis, Jeff Dennison, Bill Douglas, Benny Ertel, Chris Haid, Sheri Herrmann, Brooke Hondros, Eddie Jarvis, Donald Lynch, Carol Mears, Shelly Nunn, Bill Passwater, Heather Petry, Jennifer Powell, J.R. Rhodes, Bell Sadler, Rodney Sexton, Sandy Simerlein, Kacey Spears, Paige Strickland, Leona Taylor, Mike Watkins, Susan Williams, Kevin Woods.

Heartfelt thanks to those special people who worked behind the scenes and gave us the support needed to help us make this book a success – Jennifer Ahlers, Dina Dembicki, Bud Denker, Angel Fultz, Beth Hardy, Charlie Keiger, Philip Lyons, Amy McCauley, Karen McGee, Bob McIntosh, Lori Munro, Nicole Schopflin and Rob Burchfield, Mary Svanson, Jennifer White, Rob Wick, Uncle Bill.

We would like to show our appreciation for all the people who supported us along the way – Lenny Batycki, Adele Goodman, Joe Ley, Sandy Marshall, Don Miller, Roger Penske, Colleen Peter, Darlene De Rosa Pressley, Tanya Taylor, Deb Williams, NASCAR, and everyone at Penske Racing.

A very special thanks to Louis Upkins for giving us wings.

We offer our gratitude to the humane societies who provided beautiful shelter animals for photo shoots: Humane Society of Catawba County (Hickory, North Carolina); Humane Society of Concord & Cabarrus County (Concord, North Carolina); Iredell County Humane Society (Statesville, North Carolina); Cascades Humane Society (Jackson, Michigan).

We feel that it is important to thank you – the NASCAR fans who are supporting this project by purchasing *Pit Road Pets*. Fans are the driving force behind the growing and exciting sport of NASCAR.

We would like to thank Kodak for donating the film for this project. Kodak provided us with professional, high quality film that beautifully captured these NASCAR families with their pets.

A special thanks to our media friends featured in the book: Claire B. Lang, Larry McReynolds, Benny Parsons, Craig Reynolds, Darrell Waltrip, Matt Yocum.

A huge thank you to Michelle and Rob Croom of Ryan Newman Motorsports for their endless energy, knowledge and invaluable friendship. What a great team you are!

Yours truly,
The Pet Sisters ~ Krissie, Karen, Laura
and Rosalie, *Pit Road Pets*™

Kodak

Acknowledgements

*We would both like to give our deepest thanks to Theresa and Joe Diffie for
all you have done for us and the animals. Mona and Little Jimmy Dickens,
your gracious gift of time and energy is greatly appreciated.*

Karen Will Rogers would like to personally thank...

Our Heavenly Father. My mom, who fueled my dreams with love and true support. My dad, who will see this book from Heaven – you are missed and loved so much. My family for always giving lots of love and support: the Williams – Robert, John, Billy, Lori, Thuy, Brittany, Christopher, Ashley and Johnny; and my Uncle Dan and Aunt Margaret Grady, Aunt Donna and Uncle Ted Vargo, and Aunt Sharon. John Zoppa – you are missed. My best to Mickey Bryant. I feel so very blessed to have created this book with Krissie and Ryan Newman and Rosalie De Fini. Thanks to Rose Hein, Tracy Williams, Brandon Giles (you are always there), Ashley Giles, Travis and Delores Giles, Carol and Billy Roach, Robert Weedman, photographer Larry Hill, Stacy Williams, Holly Hefner, Ty Herndon, Mike Wolf, and David Nuding. I will always be thankful to Mickie Nuding of Simon and Schuster, Harris Gilbert, Tisha and Craig Reynolds, Lisa and Junior Johnson, Terri and Benny Parsons, Willie Kahne, Dale Forbis, Mike Kumbalbk, Paul McKelvey at Dury's Professional Photographic Supplies in Nashville, Liorah Johnson from OohLaLa Boutique in Nashville, Karen Russell, Mary Lou Cathy, Kathi Atwood, Marie Stewart, Steve Rose, Chromatics Photo Lab, Dr. Jim Coleman, Dina Dembicki, Philip Lyon, Chad D. Vander Wert, Sharon Corbitt, and Troi Hayes. Laura Lacy, ohlala, this project has been an unforgettable experience!

Laura Lacy would like to personally thank...

My parents, Bettie and Jim Lacy, for their love, guidance, advice and support. My sister, Claudia Lacy Kelly, for being a constant source of inspiration. Donna Dixon Aykroyd, my best friend and rock. Tanya Tucker for helping me grow wings. Diane and Peter Nesbitt, many thanks, and Peter thanks for a great title for the book. To all my friends for love, support and help: Bonnie Hadden, Lisa Manning, Lucy Scott, Kathy Walker, Charlie Daniels Jr., Jason Malcom, Tom Ritter, Waylon Duncan, Dale Forbis.

To Bruce Witucki, you are and always will be one in a trillion, there will never be another. Rosalie De Fini, you are awesome, we couldn't have done it without you. Many thanks! Special thanks to Larry McReynolds, Lisa and Junior Johnson, Tisha and Craig Reynolds, and Terri and Benny Parsons for being so wonderful to us. Lucy Belle Lacy, thank you for being my constant on earth and in heaven. Karen Will Rogers, the best business partner ever. I love ya girl!!! To Krissie and Ryan Newman, many thanks for your vision, commitment and energy. It has been an honor and a privilege to work with you both – such a fine and dedicated couple with a strong focus. The cause has been motivation for us as a team and a passion for us all as individuals. Your voice will be heard and the world will become a better place as a result of it. Thank you both.

Special thanks to our attorneys Philip Lyon, Bob McIntosh and Rob Wick.

About the Photographer
Karen Will Rogers

Karen Will Rogers, a professional photographer, owns and operates the Karen Will Rogers Photography Studio in Nashville, Tennessee (www.karenwillrogers.net). After leaving Los Angeles 10 years ago, she started her own photography business with a focus on music and entertainment clients, portraits, models, fine art, weddings and commercial photography.

With a soulful eye and a passion for animals, Rogers uses her talent with the camera to capture the relationships between people and their pets, creating timeless images of their bonds. She did all the photography for a previously published book, *Music Row Dogs and Nashville Cats: Country Stars and Their Pets*, released by Simon and Schuster.

Rogers has been living in North Carolina to shoot the photography for *Pit Road Pets*, and in doing so has developed a new love for racing. As she says, "I believe it's essential to be the voice for the animals to help send the message to honor our pets, because they are gifts; and to stop excess pet litters, because the truth is that they all don't get homes."

Photo by Larry Hill, Nashville, TN

About the Writer
Laura Lacy

On the fast track of the entertainment speedway, Laura Lacy has worked with movie stars, country music stars and NASCAR stars to learn about their love of pets. A native Virginian, Lacy comes to this project by way of New York, Los Angeles and Nashville, where she ran her own event planning company for executives and celebrities. Lacy has held diverse positions in the entertainment industry, including assistant to the stars, art direction and production, and now writing her second book about the furry and the famous, all for "the cause." As Lacy says, "We have beautiful animals in shelters that need loving homes. These generous celebrities will help us make a difference because they care, and they have a voice that can be heard."

Lacy and Rogers have teamed up on two projects to date: *Music Row Dogs and Nashville Cats: Country Stars and Their Pets* (Simon & Schuster 2004), and now *Pit Road Pets: NASCAR Stars and Their Pets* (Ryan Newman Foundation, 2006). As always, Lacy credits Lucy, her Chow of 13 years, for her inspiration and dedication to what she believes to be the most wonderful cause ever: the love of a pet. 🐾

About the
Ryan Newman Foundation

by Executive Director Rosalie De Fini

Two years ago, I was working as the executive director of our local humane society when I received a phone call from Krissie Newman, member at large on my board of directors. She and Ryan had received a letter from a fan that brought tears to Krissie's eyes when she read it. The woman who wrote the letter was asking for Ryan and Krissie's help. Several years ago, the woman had opened her heart and home to a stray dog. She was not in the financial position to spay her dog, but she gave her pet a loving home. Soon the dog became pregnant, and this compassionate woman now had the responsibility of caring for a litter of dogs she could not afford. Dogs from that litter later gave birth to more unwanted puppies until the brood totaled 15 dogs. She called her local animal control and veterinarians to see if any local organizations could help her vaccinate and spay/neuter the animals, but their rural community on the border of Virginia and North Carolina did not have its own no-kill humane society or public low-cost spay/neuter clinic. The woman's family did not have the means to provide veterinary care and dog food for all their dogs, so they were sharing their own groceries with their pets.

Feeling like she had nowhere else to turn and not wanting to shirk the responsibilities she and her family had accepted in caring for

The Capital Campaign for the Humane Society of Catawba County

The Humane Society of Catawba County currently operates its no-kill animal shelter from a rudimentary temporary rented facility that is comprised of a series of out-buildings and outdoor kennels in Hickory, North Carolina. Although they successfully rescue and find loving homes for a thousand animals and spay/neuter two thousand animals each year, the current facility does not pass the new North Carolina Department of Agriculture guidelines. The nonprofit organization's only hope of continuing their lifesaving work is to build a new, permanent facility. The City of Hickory donated five beautifully wooded acres on which the Humane Society is planning to build a no-kill animal shelter, education center, dog park and regional spay/neuter clinic. The low-cost public spay/neuter clinic will serve other animal rescue groups and individuals in financial need from the mountains to the piedmont of North Carolina.